Fourth Edition

HISTORY OF THE
AMERICAN PEOPLES
1840-1920
A Primary Source Reader

John Majewski | **Lisa Jacobson** | **Rana Razek**

Kendall Hunt
publishing company

Cover image © XXXX

Kendall Hunt
publishing company

www.kendallhunt.com
Send all inquiries to:
4050 Westmark Drive
Dubuque, IA 52004-1840

Copyright © 2001, 2006, 2013, 2017 by Kendall Hunt Publishing Company

ISBN 978-1-5249-1649-7

Published in the United States of America

Contents

History of the American Peoples, 1840–1920

Part III: The Conquest of the West, Reconstruction, and the Rise of Big Business

Part IV: The Progressive Era

I SELL THE SHADOW TO SUPPORT THE SUBSTANCE.

SOJOURNER TRUTH.

Part One

REPUBLICAN AMERICA, 1830–1850

Document One

Alexis de Tocqueville Marvels at the Mobile Northern Society

Context: *Alexis de Tocqueville, a French political thinker and historian, traveled throughout the United States for nine months in 1831 and published his observations two years later in* Democracy in America, *from which this excerpt is drawn. The book was translated from the original French into English in 1835 and was widely read in both the U.S. and Europe. Born into an aristocratic family, Tocqueville supported representative democracy but remained suspicious of too much equality. At the time of his visit, the United States had extended the franchise to most adult white men, commercial markets were expanding, and geographic mobility was on the rise. In this passage, de Tocqueville reflects on how economic opportunity, mobility, and democracy shaped the American character.*

Questions to Consider: *How did Tocqueville describe the American character? What did he see as the upsides and downsides of American freedom, mobility, and democracy? In your view, in what ways has the American character changed and/ or remained the same?*

In certain remote corners of the Old World you may sometimes stumble upon little places which seem to have been forgotten among the general tumult and which have stayed still while all around them moves. The inhabitants are mostly very ignorant and very poor; they take no part in affairs of government, and often governments oppress them. But yet they seem serene and often have a jovial disposition.

In America I have seen the freest and best educated of men in circumstances the happiest to be found in the world; yet it seemed to me that a cloud habitually hung on their brow, and they seemed serious and almost sad even in their pleasures.

The chief reason for this is that the former do not give a moment's thought to the ills they endure, whereas the latter never stop thinking of the good things they have not got.

It is odd to watch with what feverish ardor the Americans pursue prosperity and how they are ever tormented by the shadowy suspicion that they may not have chosen the shortest route to get it.

Americans cleave to the things of this world as if assured that they will never die, and yet are in such a rush to snatch any that come within their reach, as if expecting to stop living before they have relished them. They clutch everything but hold nothing fast, and so lose grip as they hurry after some new delight.

An American will build a house in which to pass his old age and sell it before the roof is on; he will plant a garden and rent it just as the trees are coming into bearing; he will clear a field and leave others to reap the harvest; he will take up a profession and leave it, settle in one place and soon go off elsewhere with his changing desires. If his private business allows him a moment's relaxation, he will plunge at once into the whirlpool of politics. Then, if at the end of a year crammed with work he has a little spare leisure, his restless curiosity goes with him traveling up and down the vast territories of the United States. Thus he will travel five hundred miles in a few days as a distraction from his happiness.

Death steps in in the end and stops him before he has grown tired of this futile pursuit of that complete felicity which always escapes him.

At first sight there is something astonishing in this spectacle of so many lucky men restless in the midst of abundance. But it is a spectacle as old as the world; all that is new is to see a whole people performing in it.

The taste for physical pleasures must be regarded as the first cause of this secret restlessness betrayed by the actions of the Americans, and of the inconstancy of which they give daily examples.

A man who has set his heart on nothing but the good things of this world is always in a hurry, for he has only a limited time in which to find them, get them, and enjoy them. . . .

When all prerogatives of birth and fortune are abolished, when all professions are open to all and a man's own energies may bring him to the top of any of them, an ambitious man may think it easy to launch on a great career and feel that he is called to no common destiny. But that is a delusion which experience quickly corrects. The same equality which allows each man to entertain vast hopes makes each man by himself weak. His power is limited on every side, though his longings may wander where they will.

Not only are men powerless by themselves, but at every step they find immense obstacles which they had not at first noticed.

They have abolished the troublesome privileges of some of their fellows, but they come up against the competition of all. . . . No matter how a people strives for it, all the conditions of life can never be perfectly equal. Even if, by misfortune, such an absolute dead level were attained, there would still be inequalities of intelligence which, coming directly from God, will ever escape the laws of man. . . .

Among democratic peoples men easily obtain a certain equality, but they will never get the sort of equality they long for. That is a quality which ever retreats before them without getting quite out of sight, and as it retreats it beckons them on to pursue. Every instant they think they will catch it, and each time it slips through their fingers. They see it close enough to know its charms, but they do not get near enough to enjoy it, and they will be dead before they have fully relished its delights.

Document Two

"White Slavery" Threatens the Urban North

Context: *During the 1830s and 1840s, the two major political parties both saw great promise in the material advances afforded by the expanding commercial economy, but each party supported different economic policies. While the Democratic Party favored free trade and opposed protective tariffs, the Whig Party favored protective tariffs because they raised the prices of foreign goods and gave fledgling domestic manufacturers a competitive advantage. In the 1840s Americans began using the term "white slave" to describe both female prostitutes and low-wage male laborers, many of them recent immigrants from Ireland and Central Europe. The editorial below appeared in the* United States Democratic Review, *a northern journal that both shaped and reflected the attitudes of many Democratic Party voters.*

Questions to Consider: *How did the* United States Democratic Review *editorial assess the impact of commercial development on economic mobility and democratic values? How did the journal's assessment differ from Tocqueville's? How did the journal link the expanding commercial economy to the formation of an American national identity?*

The *United States Democratic Review* Argues That "White Slavery" Threatenes The Urban North (1842)

The main question discussed in all the works on political economy ... within the last twenty years, relates to the best means of ameliorating the condition of the laboring population; ... while wealth has increased in certain quarters, poverty has not been proportionately diminished in others. ...

The poverty to which we allude, is that wholesale pestilence, which is now considered as a natural grade in society and which makes perpetual calls on the legislator and the magistrate to satisfy its ceaseless cravings. It is the sure inheritance of the *White Slave* of the factory and of the coal-mine, who in the midst of the most dazzling social improvements and political ameliorations, still continues to trudge on from morning till night for the bare privilege of living—without even so much as a prospective termination to the period of his revolting bondage. ...

[T]he almost unbroken tide of progressive amelioration has made us the freest, and may yet make us the wealthiest and most refined society of modern ages. But still the condition of the peasantry and the laboring population of the manufacturing districts is yet strongly susceptible of improvement. The present clamors of the Whig party to favor and foster the factory system among us are fraught with direful mischief. With the high price of labor that exists in the United States—with our scanty supply of moneyed capital—with our unlimited range of uncultivated or half-improved soil—it is almost a crime against society to divert human industry from the fields and the forests to iron forges and cotton factories. Nature has pointed out the course which we ought to pursue for perhaps half a century to come, till the plough and the spade have followed the axe of the woodcutter into their "primeval wilderness of shade," and till happy plantations shall have been formed on the deserted domains of the Indian huntsman from the Atlantic to the Ohio, and from the Mississippi to the Pacific. She has directed us to cling to the bosom of mother Earth, as to the most fertile source of wealth, and the most abundant reward of labor. She has told us to remain planters, farmers, and wood-cutters—to extend society and cultivation to new regions—to practice and improve the arts of the builder, the carpenter, and the naval architect—to facilitate every means of internal communication—to promote every branch of internal trade—to encourage every variety of landed produce, but not to waste the energies of our labor; or to interrupt the course of our prosperity, by forcing at home the manufacture of articles which foreigners could supply at half the price for which they could be made in America. . . .

[W]e are well aware that in point of humane treatments, rate of wages, and moral restrictions, our factory system is far superior to that which is the shame and degradation of England:— we are also willing to acknowledge that there are occasionally startling instances of prosperity and happiness growing out of early initiation into these dens of toil and trouble: but it does not require a great deal of penetration to perceive that, notwithstanding these negative advantages, the principles of WHITE SLAVERY are gradually taking root in the very midst of us. . . .

There is a class writers, who . . . have undertaken a crusade against Adam Smith and his followers, averring that the modern school of political economy is based on erroneous principles, that the system of protective duties established by our ancestors was the consummation of human wisdom,—and that it is not merely the right, but the duty of a state to determine in what channels capital should flow, and toward what objects industry should be directed. . . .

Protections and monopolies are not only evils, but they are evils that love to perpetuate themselves. To establish them is easy enough; but to remove them has been the most difficult task that modern statesmen have had to encounter.

Name: _____ Date: _____

Document Analysis Worksheet

1. Date/Author of Document/Author's Position: Intended Audience:

2. Why was this document written? List three points the author made that you find important.

3. List two things the document tells you about life in the United States at the time it was written.

4. Write a question to the author that the document left unanswered.

Name: _____ Date: _____

Comparative Analysis Worksheet

Choose two documents from this week's readings in which the document authors present different takes on a particular issue.

    1. Identify two or three key points on which the authors agree and/or disagree.

_____

_____

_____

_____

_____

    2. Develop your analysis of these two documents further by answering one or two questions listed in the "Questions to Consider" section for each document.

_____

_____

_____

_____

_____

_____

_____

_____

_____

_____

Document Three

Godey's Lady's Book Promotes Domestic Ideology

Context: *During the first half of the nineteenth century, scores of advice books, women's magazines, and sentimental novels outlined the tenets of domestic ideology. Domestic ideology held that women possessed talents and virtues best suited for the home, while men's nature and talents best suited them to preside over the public sphere of business and politics. In contrast to men, who were often portrayed as cold, calculating, and competitive, women were viewed as naturally pious, sentimental, and caring.* Godey's Lady's Book *was a particularly well-known exponent of domestic ideology. Under the leadership of publisher Louis Godey and editor Sarah Hale,* Godey's Lady's Book *had 150,000 subscribers in 1860, which made it the most popular magazine in the United States. Much like domestic ideology itself, the magazine catered to northern middle-class women.*

Questions to Consider: *Why did* Godey's Lady's Book *contend that men and women were best suited to preside over different "spheres"? In what ways did domestic ideology limit women's power within society? In what ways might women use domestic ideology to exert more influence in political and social matters? In what ways do the selections from the magazine suggest that nineteenth-century Americans were concerned about the strength of republican "virtue" in their society?*

"Female Education" (December 1830)

A YOUNG lady may excel in speaking French and Italian; may repeat a few passages from the volume of extracts; play like a professor, and sing like a siren; have her dressing-room decorated with her own drawing tables, stands, flower pots, screens and cabinets; nay, she may dance like Semphronia herself, and yet we shall insist, that she may have been very badly educated. I am far from meaning to set no value whatever on any or all of these qualifications; they are all of them elegant, and many of them tend to the perfecting of a polite education. These things, in their measure and degree may be done; but there are others which should not be left undone. Many things are becoming, but "one thing is needful." Besides, as the world seems to be fully apprised of the value of whatever tends to embellish life, there is less occasion here to insist on its importance. But, though a well-bred young lady may lawfully learn most of the fashionable arts, yet, let me ask, does it seem to be the true end of education, to make women of fashion dancers, singers, players, painters, actresses, sculptors, gilders, varnishers, engravers, and embroiderers?

Most men are commonly destined to some profession, and their minds are, consequently, turned each to its respective object. Would it not be strange if they were called out to exercise their profession, or set up their trade, with only a little general knowledge of the trades and professions of all other men, and without any previous definite application to their own peculiar calling? The profession of ladies, to which the bent of their instruction should be turned, is that of daughters, wives, mothers, and mistresses of families. They should be, therefore, trained with a view to these several conditions, and be furnished with ideas, and principles, and qualifications, and habits, ready to be applied and appropriated, as occasion may demand, to each of these respective situations.

Though the arts; which merely embellish life, must claim admiration, when a man of sense comes to marry, it is a companion whom he wants, and not an artist. It is not merely a creature who can paint and play, and sing, and draw, and dress, and dance: it is a being who can comfort and counsel him; one who can reason, and reflect, and feel, and judge, and discourse, and discriminate; one who can assist him in his affairs, lighten his cares, soothe his sorrows, purify his joys, strengthen his principles, and educate his children. Such is the woman who is fit for a wife, a mother, and a mistress of a family.

Editors' Table (1851)

Now, 1851 finds "the whole world kin," as it were, busy in preparing for such an Industrial Convention as was never held since time began [London's Crystal Palace Exhibition]. What trophies of mind and might will be there exhibited! Not victories won by force or fraud, with their advantages appropriated to exalt a few individuals; but real advances made in those arts which give the means of improvement to nations, and add to the knowledge, freedom, and happiness of the people!

We are not intending to enlarge on this theme, which will be better done by abler pens. We only allude to it here, in order to draw the attention of our readers to one curious fact, which those who are aiming to place women in the workshop, to compete with men, should consider: namely, that none, or very few specimens of female ingenuity or industry will be found in the world's great show-shop. The female mind has as yet manifested very little of the kind of genius termed mechanical, or inventive. Nor is it the lack of learning which has caused this uniform lack of constructive talent. Many ignorant men have studied out and made curious inventions of mechanical skill; women never. We are constrained to say we do not believe woman would ever have invented the compass, the printing-press, the steam-engine, or even a loom. The difference between the mental power of the two sexes, as it is distinctly traced in Holy Writ and human history, we have described and illustrated in a work soon to be published. We trust this will prove of importance in settling the question of what woman's province really is, and where her station should be in the onward march of civilization. It is not mechanical, but moral power which is now needed. That woman was endowed with moral goodness superior to that possessed by man is the doctrine of the Bible; and this moral power she must be trained to use for the promotion of goodness, and purity, and holiness in men. There is no need that she should help him in his task of subduing the world. He has the strong arm and the ingenious mind to understand and grapple with things of earth; but he needs her aid in subduing himself, his own selfish passions, and animal propensities.

To sum up the matter, the special gifts of God to men are mechanical ingenuity and physical strength. To women He has given moral insight or instinct, and the patience that endures physical suffering. Both sexes equally need enlightenment of mind or reason by education, in order to make their peculiar gifts of the greatest advantage to themselves, to each other, to the happiness and improvement of society, and to the glory of God.

Such are the principles which we have been striving to disseminate for the last twenty years; and we rejoice, on this jubilee day of the century, that our work has been crowned with good success, and that the prospect before us is bright and cheering. The wise king of Israel asserted the power and predicted the future of woman in these remarkable words, "Strength and honor are her clothing; and she shall rejoice in time to come." And so it will be. But the elevation of the sex will not consist in becoming like man, in doing man's work, or striving for the dominion of the world. The true woman cannot work with materials of earth, build up cities, mould marble forms, or discover new mechanical inventions to aid physical improvement. She has a higher and holier vocation. She works in the elements of human nature; her orders of architecture are formed in the soul. Obedience, temperance, truth, love, piety, these she must build up in the character of her children. Often, too, she is called to repair the ravages and beautify the waste places which sin, care, and the desolating storms of life leave in the mind and heart of the husband she reverences and obeys. This task she should perform faithfully, but with humility, remembering that it was for woman's sake Eden was forfeited, because Adam loved his wife more than his Creator, and that man's nature has to contend with a degree of depravity, or temptation to sin, which the female, by the grace of God, has never experienced. Yes, the wife is dependent on her husband for the position she holds in society; she must rely on him for protection and support; she should look up to him with reverence as her earthly guardian, the "saviour of the body," as St. Paul says, and be obedient. Does any wife say her husband is not worthy of this honor? Then render it to the office with which God has invested him as head of the family; but use your privilege of motherhood so to train your son that he may be worthy of this reverence and obedience from his wife. Thus through your sufferings the world may be made better; every faithful performance of private duty adds to the stock of public virtues.

We trust, before the sands of this century are run out, that these Bible truths will be the rule of faith and of conduct with every American wife and mother, and that the moral influence of American women will be felt and blessed as the saving power not only of our nation, but of the world. Our hopes are high, not only because we believe our principles are true, but because we expect to be sustained and helped by all who are true and right-minded.

Document Four

Sarah Grimké Calls for Greater Equality

Context: *While most middle-class women accepted the dictates of domestic ideology, a few radical reformers rejected it. Sarah and Angelina Grimké were from a wealthy South Carolina family that owned many slaves. When visiting Philadelphia, Pennsylvania, in 1819, Sarah converted to Quakerism, a religion that stressed plain dress, orderly habits, and individual conscience. Some years later she convinced Angelina to convert as well. Although the Quakers were a relatively small religious group, their unwavering opposition to slavery made them extremely influential in the abolitionist movement. The Grimkés became speakers for the American Anti-Slavery Society and advocates of women's rights.*

Questions to Consider: *What specific reforms did Sarah Grimké advocate to improve the condition of women in the United States? Did her arguments completely dismiss domestic ideology, or did she merely seek to reform it? How did Grimké use religion to argue for greater equality? Why do you think she focused so much of her letter on slave women? What do you make of Grimké's closing words: "Thine in the bonds of womanhood"?*

Sarah M. Grimké, "On the Condition of Women in the United States" (Brookline, 1837)

My Dear Sister,

. . . During the early part of my life, my lot was cast among the butterflies of the fashionable world; and of this class of women, I am constrained to say, both from experience and observation, that their education is miserably deficient; that they are taught to regard marriage as the one thing needful, the only avenue to distinction; hence to attract the notice and win the attentions of men, by their external charms, is the chief business of fashionable girls. They seldom think that men will be allured by intellectual acquirements, because they find, that where any mental superiority exists, a woman is generally shunned and regarded as stepping out of her "appropriate sphere," which, in their view, is to dress, to dance, to set out to the best possible advantage her person, to read the novels which inundate the press, and which do more to destroy her character as a rational creature, than any thing else. Fashionable women regard themselves, and are regarded by men, as pretty toys or as mere instruments of pleasure; and the vacuity of mind, the heartlessness, the frivolity, which is the necessary result of this false and debasing estimate of women, can only be fully understood by those who have mingled in the folly and wickedness of fashionable life; and who have been called from such pursuits by the voice of the lord Jesus, inviting their weary and heavy laden souls to come unto Him and learn of Him, that they may find something worthy of their immortal spirit, and their intellectual powers; that they may learn the high and holy purposes of their creation, and consecrate themselves unto the service of God; and not, as is now the case, to the pleasure of man.

There is another and much more numerous class in this country, who are withdrawn by education or circumstances from the circle of fashionable amusements, but who are brought up with the dangerous and absurd idea, that marriage is a kind of preferment; and that to be able to keep their husband's house, and render his situation comfortable, is the end of her being. Much that she does and says and thinks is done in reference to this situation; and to be married is too often held up to the view of girls as the sine qua non of human happiness and human existence. For this purpose more than for any other, I verily believe the majority of girls are trained. This is demonstrated by the imperfect education which is bestowed upon them, and the little pains taken to cultivate their minds, after they leave school, by the little time allowed them for reading, and by the idea being constantly inculcated, that although all household concerns should be attended to with scrupulous punctuality at particular seasons, the improvement of their intellectual capacities is only a secondary consideration, and may serve as an occupation to fill up the odds and ends of time. In most families, it is considered a matter of far more consequence to call a girl off from making a pie, or a pudding, than to interrupt her whilst engaged in her studies. This mode of training necessarily exalts, in their view, the animal above the intellectual and spiritual nature, and teaches women to regard themselves as a kind of machinery, necessary to keep the domestic engine in order, but of little value as the intelligent companions of men.

Let no one think, from these remarks, that I regard a knowledge of housewifery as beneath the acquisition of women. Far from it: I believe that a complete knowledge of household affairs is an indispensable requisite in a woman's education,—that by the mistress of a family, whether married or single, doing her duty thoroughly and understandingly, the happiness of the family is increased to an incalculable degree, as well as a vast amount of time and money saved. All I complain of is, that our education consists so almost exclusively in culinary and other manual operations. I do long to see the time, when it will no longer be necessary for women to expend so many precious hours in furnishing "a well spread table," but that their husbands will forego some of their accustomed indulgences in this way, and encourage their wives to devote some portion of their time to mental cultivation, even at the expense of having to dine sometimes on baked potatoes, or bread and butter. . . .

The influence of women over the minds and character of children of both sexes, is allowed to be far greater than that of men. This being the case by the very ordering of nature, women should be prepared by education for the performance of their sacred duties as mothers and as sisters. . . .

There is another way in which the general opinion, that women are inferior to men, is manifested, that bears with tremendous effect on the laboring class, and indeed on almost all who are obligate to earn a subsistence, whether it be by mental or physical exertion—I allude to the disproportionate value set on the time and labor of men and of women. A man who is engaged in teaching, can always, I believe, command a higher price for tuition than a woman—even when he teaches the same branches, and is not in any respect superior to the woman. This I know is the case in boarding and other schools with which I have been acquainted, and it is so in every occupation in which the sexes engage indiscriminately. As for example, in tailoring, a man has twice, or three times as much for making a waistcoat or pantaloons as a woman, although the work done by each may be equally good. In those employments which are peculiar to women, their time is estimated at only half the value of that of men. A woman who goes out to wash, works as hard in proportion as a wood sawyer, or a coal heaver, but she is not generally able to make more than half as much by a day's work. . . . I have known a widow, left with four or five children to provide for, unable to leave home because her helpless babes demand her attention, compelled to earn a scanty subsistence, by making coarse shirts at 12-½ cents a piece, or by taking in washing, for which she was paid by some wealthy persons 12-½ cents per dozen. All these things evince the low estimation in which woman is held. There is yet another and more disastrous consequence arising from this unscriptural notion—women being educated, from earliest childhood, to regard themselves as inferior creatures, have not that self-respect which conscious equality would engender, and hence when their virtue is assailed, they yield to temptation with facility, under the idea that it rather exalts than debases them, to be connected with a superior being.

There is another class of women in this country, to whom I cannot refer, without feelings of the deepest shame and sorrow. I allude to our female slaves. Our southern cities are wheeled beneath a tide of pollution; the virtue of female slaves is wholly at the mercy of irresponsible tyrants, and women are bought and sold in our slave markets, to gratify the brute lust of those who bear the name of Christian. In our slave States, if amid all her degradation and ignorance, a woman desires to preserve her virtue unsullied, she is either bribed or whipped into compliance, or if she dares resist her seducer, her life by the laws of some of the slave States may be, and has actually been sacrificed to the fury of the disappointed passion. Where such laws do not exist, the power which is necessarily vested in the master over his property, leaves the defenseless slave entirely at his mercy, and the suffering of some females on this account, both physical and mental, are intense. Mr. Gholson, in the House of Delegates of Virginia, in 1832, said, "He really had been under the impression that he owned his slaves. He had lately purchased four women and ten children, in whom he thought he had obtained a great bargain; for he supposed they were his own property, as were his brood mares." But even if any laws existed in the United States, as in Athens formerly, for the protection of female slaves, they would be null and void, because the evidence of a colored person is not admitted against a white, in any of our Courts of Justice in the slave States. "In Athens, if a female slave had cause to complain of any want of respect to the laws of modesty, she could seek the protection of the temple, and demand a change of owners; and such appeals were never discountenanced, or neglected by the magistrates." In Christian America, the slave has no refuge from unbridled cruelty and lust.

S. A. Forrall, speaking of the state of morals at the South, says, "Negresses when young and lively, are often employed by the planter, or his friends, to administer to their sensual desires. This frequently is a matter of speculation, for if the offspring, a mulatto, be a handsome female, 800 or 1000 dollars may be obtained for her in the New Orleans market. It is an occurrence of no uncommon nature to see a Christian father sell his own daughter, and the brother his own sister." . . . I will add but one more from the numerous testimonies respecting the degradation of female slaves, and the licentiousness of the South. It is from the Circular of the Kentucky Union, for the moral and religious improvement of the colored race. "To the female character among our black population, we cannot allude but with feeling of the bitterest shame. A similar condition of moral pollution and utter disregard of a pure and virtuous reputation, is to be found only without the pale of Christendom. That such a state of society should exist in a Christian nation, claiming to be the most enlightened upon the earth, without calling forth any particular attention to its existence, though ever before our eyes and in our families, is a moral phenomenon at once unaccountable and disgraceful."

Nor does the colored woman suffer alone: the moral purity of the white woman is deeply contaminated. In the daily habit of seeing the virtue of her enslaved sister sacrificed without hesitancy or remorse, she looks upon the crimes of seduction and illicit intercourse without horror, and although not personally involved in the guilt, she loses that value for innocence in her own, as well as the other sex, which is one of the strongest safeguards to virtue. She lives in habitual intercourse with men, whom she knows to be polluted by licentiousness, and often is she compelled to witness in her own domestic circle, those disgusting and heart-sickening jealousies and strifes which disgraced and distracted the family of Abraham. In addition to all this, the female slaves suffer every species of degradation and cruelty, which the most wanton barbarity can inflict; they are indecently divested of their clothing, sometimes tied up and severely whipped, sometimes prostrated on the earth, while their naked bodies are torn by the scorpion lash.

> *The whip on WOMAN's shrinking flesh!*
> *Our soil yet reddening with the stains*
> *Caught from her scourging warm and fresh.*

Can any American woman look at these scenes of shocking licentiousness and cruelty, and fold her hands in apathy and say, "I have nothing to do with slavery"? She cannot and be guiltless.

I cannot close this letter, without saying a few words on the benefits to be derived by men, as well as women, from the opinions I advocate relative to the equality of the sexes. Many women are now supported, in idleness and extravagance, by the industry of their husbands, fathers, or brothers, who are compelled to toil out their existence, at the counting house, or in the printing office, or some other laborious occupation, while the wife and daughters and sisters take no part in the support of the family, and appear to think that their sole business is to spend the hard bought earnings of their male friends. I deeply regret such a state of things, because I believe that if women felt their responsibility, for the support of themselves, or their families it would add strength and dignity to their characters, and teach them more true sympathy for their husbands, than is now generally manifested,—a sympathy which would be exhibited by actions as well as words. Our brethren may reject my doctrine, because it runs counter to common opinions, and because it wounds their pride; but I believe they would be "partakers of the benefit" resulting from the Equality of the Sexes, and would find that woman, as their equal, was unspeakably more valuable than woman as their inferior, both as a moral and an intellectual being.

Thine in the bonds of womanhood,

Sarah M. Grimké

Document Five

The Seneca Falls Convention Advocates Complete Equality

Context: *Elizabeth Cady Stanton and Lucretia Mott were among two of the women excluded from an abolitionist conference held in London in 1840. They vowed to organize their own conference that would advance the cause of women's rights. Eight years later, they succeeded in organizing a highly successful conference in Seneca Falls, New York. Although many luminaries of the abolitionist movement attended the convention—including the black abolitionist Frederick Douglass—Stanton and Mott were the key organizers. The Seneca Falls conference launched the women's rights movement based on complete equality, including the particularly radical demand of women's suffrage.*

Questions to Consider: *Why did Stanton choose the form of the Declaration of Independence to state her position? What specific assumptions of domestic ideology did Stanton attack? Why did the call for women's right to vote generate the most heated debate among the delegates? In what ways does the document reveal the racial and class biases of its chief authors?*

Declaration of Sentiments (1848)

When, in the course of human events, it becomes necessary for one portion of the family of man to assume among the people of the earth a position different from that which they have hitherto occupied, but one to which the laws of nature and of nature's God entitle them, a decent respect to the opinions of mankind requires that they should declare the causes that impel them to such a course.

We hold these truths to be self-evident: that all men and women are created equal; that they are endowed by their Creator with certain inalienable rights, that among these are life, liberty, and the pursuit of happiness; that to secure these rights governments are instituted, deriving their just powers from the consent of the governed. Whenever any form of government becomes destructive of these ends, it is the right of those who suffer from it to refuse allegiance to it, and to insist upon the institution of a new government, laying its foundation on such principles, and organizing its powers in such form as to them shall seem most likely to effect their safety and happiness. Prudence, indeed, will dictate that governments long established should not be changed for light and transient causes; and accordingly, all experience hath shown that mankind are more disposed to suffer, while evils are sufferable, than to right themselves by abolishing the forms to which they were accustomed. But when a long train of abuses and usurpations, pursuing invariably the same object evinces a design to reduce them under absolute despotism, it is their duty to throw off such government, and to provide new guards for their future security. Such has been the patient sufferance of the women under this government, and such is now the necessity which constrains them to demand the equal station to which they are entitled.

The history of mankind is a history of repeated injuries and usurpations on the part of man toward woman, having in direct object the establishment of an absolute tyranny over her. To prove this, let facts be submitted to a candid world.

He has never permitted her to exercise her inalienable right to the elective franchise.

He has compelled her to submit to laws, in the formation of which she had no voice.

He has withheld from her rights which are given to the most ignorant and degraded men both natives and foreigners.

Having deprived her of this first right of a citizen, the elective franchise, thereby leaving her without representation in the halls of legislation, he has oppressed her on all sides.

He has made her, if married, in the eye of the law, civilly dead.

He has taken from her all right in property, even to the wages she earns.

He has made her, morally, an irresponsible being, as she can commit many crimes with impunity, provided they be done in the presence of her husband. In the covenant of marriage, she is compelled to promise obedience to her husband, he becoming, to all intents and purposes, her master—the law giving him power to deprive her of her liberty, and to administer chastisement.

He has so framed the laws of divorce, as to what shall be the proper causes of divorce; in case of separation, to whom the guardianship of the children shall be given; as to be wholly regardless of the happiness of women—the law, in all cases, going upon a false supposition of the supremacy of man, and giving all power into his hands.

After depriving her of all rights as a married woman, if single and the owner of property, he has taxed her to support a government which recognizes her only when her property can be made profitable to it.

He has monopolized nearly all the profitable employments, and from those she is permitted to follow, she receives but a scanty remuneration.

He closes against her all the avenues to wealth and distinction, which he considers most honorable to himself. As a teacher of theology, medicine, or law, she is not known.

He has denied her the facilities for obtaining a thorough education—all colleges being closed against her.

He allows her in Church, as well as State, but a subordinate position, claiming Apostolic authority for her exclusion from the ministry, and, with some exceptions, from any public participation in the affairs of the Church.

He has created a false public sentiment, by giving to the world a different code of morals for men and women, by which moral delinquencies which exclude women from society, are not only tolerated but deemed of little account in man.

He has usurped the prerogative of Jehovah himself, claiming it as his right to assign for her a sphere of action, when that belongs to her conscience and to her God.

He has endeavored, in every way that he could, to destroy her confidence in her own powers, to lessen her self-respect, and to make her willing to lead a dependent and abject life.

Now, in view of this entire disfranchisement of one-half the people of this country, their social and religious degradation, in view of the unjust laws above mentioned, and because women do feel themselves aggrieved, oppressed, and fraudulently deprived of their most sacred rights, we insist that they have immediate admission to all the rights and privileges which belong to them as citizens of the United States.

In entering upon the great work before us, we anticipate no small amount of misconception, misrepresentation, and ridicule; but we shall use every instrumentality within our power to effect our object. We shall employ agents, circulate tracts, petition the state and national legislatures, and endeavor to enlist the pulpit and the press in our behalf. We hope this Convention will be followed by a series of Conventions, embracing every part of the country.

Firmly relying upon the final triumph of the Right and the True, we do this day affix our signatures to this declaration.

Lucretia Mott, Elizabeth Cady Stanton, Eunice Newton Foote, Mary Ann McClintock, Martha C. Wright, Jane C. Hunt, Amy Post, Catharine A. F. Stebbins, Mary H. Hallowell, Charlotte Woodward, Sarah Hallowell

Richard P Hunt, Samuel D. Tilman, Elisha Foote, Frederick Douglass, Elias J. Doty, James Mott, Thomas McClintock

This Declaration was unanimously adopted and signed by 32 men and 68 women.

Resolutions

Whereas the great precept of nature is conceded to be, "that man shall pursue his own true and substantial happiness." Blackstone, in his Commentaries, remarks, that this law of Nature being coeval with mankind, and dictated by God himself, is of course superior in obligation to any other. It is binding over all the globe, in all countries, and at all times; no human laws are of any validity if contrary to this, and such of them as are valid, derive all their force, and all their validity, and all their authority, mediately and immediately, from this original; therefore,

Resolved, That such laws as conflict, in any way, with the true and substantial happiness of woman, are contrary to the great precept of nature, and of no validity; for this is "superior in obligation to any other."

Resolved, That all laws which prevent woman from occupying such a station in society as her conscience shall dictate, or which place her in a position inferior to that of man, are contrary to the great precept of nature, and therefore of no force or authority.

Resolved, That woman is man's equal—was intended to be so by the Creator—and the highest good of the race demands that she should be recognized as such.

Resolved, That the women of this country ought to be enlightened in regard to the laws under which they live, that they may no longer publish their degradation, by declaring themselves satisfied with their present position, nor their ignorance, by asserting that they have all the rights they want.

Resolved, That inasmuch as man, while claiming for himself intellectual superiority, does accord to woman moral superiority, it is pre-eminently his duty to encourage her to speak, and teach, as she has an opportunity, in all religious assemblies.

Resolved, That the same amount of virtue, delicacy, and refinement of behavior, that is required of woman in the social state, should also be required of man, and the same transgressions should be visited with equal severity on both man and woman.

Resolved, That the objection of indelicacy and impropriety, which is so often brought against woman when she addresses a public audience, comes with a very ill-grace from those who encourage, by their attendance, her appearance on the stage, in the concert, or in feats of the circus.

Resolved, That woman has too long rested satisfied in the circumscribed limits which corrupt customs and a perverted application of the Scriptures have marked out for her, and that it is time she should move in the enlarged sphere which her great Creator has assigned her.

Resolved, That it is the duty of the women of this country to secure to themselves their sacred right to the elective franchise.

Resolved, That the equality of human rights results necessarily from the fact of the identity of the race in capabilities and responsibilities.

Resolved, therefore, That, being invested by the Creator with the same capabilities, and the same consciousness of responsibility for their exercise, it is demonstrably the right and duty of woman, equally with man, to promote every righteous cause, by every righteous means; and especially in regard to the great subjects of morals and religion, it is self-evidently her right to participate with her brother in teaching them, both in private and in public, by writing and by speaking, by any instrumentalities proper to be used, and in any assemblies proper to be held; and this being a self-evident truth, growing out of the divinely implanted principles of human nature, any custom or authority adverse to it, whether modern or wearing the hoary sanction of antiquity, is to be regarded as a self-evident falsehood, and at war with the interests of mankind.

The only resolution which met opposition was the 9th, demanding the right of suffrage which, however, after a prolonged discussion was adopted. All of the meetings throughout the two days were largely attended, but this, like every step in progress, was ridiculed from Maine to Louisiana.

Document Six

Sojourner Truth Links Women's Rights to Antislavery

Context: *Sojourner Truth (1791–1883) was an itinerant preacher, lecturer, and an advocate for the abolition of slavery, women's rights, and freedman's rights. Born into slavery Isabella Baumfree, she was emancipated by the state of New York in 1827. When her former masters refused to release her, she fled to the home of an abolitionist family where she experienced a religious conversion. At the age of 52, she changed her name to Sojourner Truth, and devoted herself to preaching the Gospel. She briefly joined a utopian community where she met abolitionists Frederick Douglass and William Lloyd Garrison, and began her public speaking career. The excerpted remarks below come from an address Truth gave to the Women's Rights convention in Akron, Ohio, on May 28, 1851.*

Questions to Consider: *Why does Truth repeatedly ask, "ain't I a woman?" What arguments does she make for extending equal rights and the franchise to all women? How does she challenge the central tenets of domestic ideology? In what ways are her arguments both similar to and different from those of her white middle-class contemporaries?*

Well, children where there is so much racket there must be something out of kilter. I think that 'twixt the negroes of the South and the women of the North, all talking about rights, the white men will be in a fix pretty soon. But what's all this here talking about?

That man over there says that women need to be helped into carriages, and lifted over ditches, and to have the best place everywhere. Nobody ever helps me into carriages or over mudpuddles, or gives me any best place! And ain't I a woman? Look at me! Look at my arm! I have ploughed and planted, and gathered into barns, and no man could head me! And ain't I a woman? I could work as much and eat as much as a man—when I could get it—and bear the lash as well! And ain't I a woman? I have borne 13 children, and seen them most all sold off to slavery, and when I cried out with my mother's grief, none but Jesus heard me! And ain't I a woman?

Then they talk about this thing in the head; what's this they call it? [Intellect, someone whispers.] That's it, honey. What's that got to do with women's rights or negro's rights? If my cup won't hold but a pint, and yours holds a quart, wouldn't you be mean not to let me have my half-measure full?

Then that little man in the back there, he says women can't have as much rights as men, 'cause Christ wasn't a woman! Where did your Christ come from? From God and a woman! Man had nothing to do with Him.

If the first woman God ever made was strong enough to turn the world upside down all alone, these women together ought to be able to turn it back, and get it right side up again! And now they is asking to do it, the men better let them.

Obliged to you for hearing me, and now old Sojourner ain't got nothing more to say.

Name: _____ Date: _____

Document Analysis Worksheet

1. Date/Author of Document/Author's Position: Intended Audience:

2. Why was this document written? List three points the author made that you find important.

3. List two things the document tells you about life in the United States at the time it was written.

4. Write a question to the author that the document left unanswered.

Name: _____ Date: _____

Comparative Analysis Worksheet

Choose two documents from this week's readings in which the document authors present different takes on a particular issue.

1. Identify two or three key points on which the authors agree and/or disagree.

_____

_____

_____

_____

_____

_____

2. Develop your analysis of these two documents further by answering one or two questions listed in the "Questions to Consider" section for each document.

_____

_____

_____

_____

_____

_____

_____

_____

_____

_____

_____

Part Two

RACE, SLAVERY, AND CIVIL WAR

Document Seven

William Lloyd Garrison Calls for the Immediate Abolition of Slavery (1831)

Context: *In the early nineteenth century, few white Americans (northerners or southerners) called for the complete abolition of slavery. While some high-profile public figures believed that slavery was a moral and economic evil, they usually supported gradual emancipation schemes that would have compensated slaveholders. William Lloyd Garrison, a young newspaper editor from New England, called for the immediate and unconditional end to slavery. He published* The Liberator—*the nation's most prominent abolitionist paper—from 1831 until 1866. Many Americans believed that Garrison and the abolitionists were dangerous radicals.*

Questions to Consider: *What key political document did Garrison cite in supporting abolitionism? Where did Garrison encounter the most opposition to abolitionism? How did Garrison intend to convince Americans of the evil of slavery?*

During my recent tour for the purpose of exciting the minds of the people by a series of discourses on the subject of slavery, every place that I visited gave fresh evidence of the fact, that a greater revolution in public sentiment was to be effected in the free States—and particularly in New-England—than at the South. I found contempt more bitter, opposition more active, detraction more relentless, prejudice more stubborn, and apathy more frozen, than among slave-owners themselves. Of course, there were individual exceptions to the contrary. This state of things afflicted, but did not dishearten me. I determined, at every hazard, to lift up the standard of emancipation in the eyes of the nation, within sight of Bunker Hill and in the birthplace of liberty [Boston, Massachusetts]. That standard is now unfurled; and long may it float, unhurt by the spoliations of time or the missiles of a desperate foe—yea, till every chain be broken, and every bondman set free! Let Southern oppressors tremble—let their secret abettors tremble— let their Northern apologists tremble—let all the enemies of the persecuted blacks tremble.

. . . In defending the great cause of human rights, I wish to derive the assistance of all religions and of all parties. Assenting to the "self-evident truth" maintained in the American Declaration of Independence, "that all men are created equal, and endowed by their Creator with certain inalienable rights—among which are life, liberty and the pursuit of happiness," I shall strenuously contend for the immediate enfranchisement of our slave population. In

Park-Street Church, on the Fourth of July, 1829, I unreflectingly assented to the popular but pernicious doctrine of gradual abolition. I seize this moment to make a full and unequivocal recantation, and thus publicly to ask pardon of my God, of my country, and of my brethren the poor slaves, for having uttered a sentiment so full of timidity, injustice, and absurdity. A similar recantation, from my pen, was published in the *Genius of Universal Emancipation* at Baltimore, in September, 1829. My conscience is now satisfied.

I am aware that many object to the severity of my language; but is there not cause for severity? I will be as harsh as truth, and as uncompromising as justice. On this subject, I do not wish to think, or to speak, or write, with moderation. No! no! Tell a man whose house is on fire to give a moderate alarm; tell him to moderately rescue his wife from the hands of the ravisher; tell the mother to gradually extricate her babe from the fire into which it has fallen;—but urge me not to use moderation in a cause like the present. I am in earnest—I will not equivocate—I will not excuse—I will not retreat a single inch—AND I WILL BE HEARD. The apathy of the people is enough to make every statue leap from its pedestal, and to hasten the resurrection of the dead.

It is pretended that I am retarding the cause of emancipation by the coarseness of my invective and the precipitancy of my measures. The charge is not true. On this question of my influence,—humble as it is,—is felt at this moment to a considerable extent, and shall be felt in coming years—not perniciously, but beneficially—not as a curse, but as a blessing; and posterity will bear testimony that I was right. I desire to thank God, that he enables me to disregard "the fear of man which bringeth a snare," and to speak His truth in its simplicity and power. And here I close with this fresh dedication:

> *"Oppression! I have seen thee, face to face,*
> *And met thy cruel eye and cloudy brow,*
> *But thy soul-withering glance I fear not now—*
> *For dread to prouder feelings doth give place*
> *Of deep abhorrence! Scorning the disgrace*
> *Of slavish knees that at thy footstool bow,*
> *I also kneel—but with far other vow*
> *Do hail thee and thy herd of hirelings base:—*
> *I swear, while life-blood warms my throbbing veins,*
> *Still to oppose and thwart, with heart and hand,*
> *Thy brutalising sway—till Afric's chains*
> *Are burst, and Freedom rules the rescued land,—*
> *Trampling Oppression and his iron rod:*
> *Such is the vow I take—SO HELP ME GOD!"*

[by the Scottish poet Thomas Pringle]

George Fitzhugh Attacks Wage Labor

Context: *As the abolitionists stepped up their attack on slavery, southerners took to the offensive. Rather than apologize for slavery, they defended the institution as a positive good, both for whites and the slaves themselves. George Fitzhugh, a slaveholder from Virginia, was one of the best-known proponents of the positive defense of slavery. Fitzhugh's attack against wage labor, in particular, provoked outrage among many northerners.*

Questions to Consider: *Why did Fitzhugh equate wage slavery with "moral cannibalism?" According to Fitzhugh, why were slaves generally happy? What economic dynamic accounted for the differences between wage laborers and slaves?*

George Fitzhugh, Cannibals All! Chapter I: The Universal Trade (1857)

We are, all, North and South, engaged in the White Slave Trade, and he who succeeds best, is esteemed most respectable. It is far more cruel than the Black Slave Trade, because it exacts more of its slaves, and neither protects nor governs them. We boast, that it exacts more, when we say, "that the profits made from employing free labor are greater than those from slave labor." The profits, made from free labor, are the amount of the products of such labor, which the employer, by means of the command which capital or skill gives him, takes away, exacts or "exploits" from the free laborer. The profits of slave labor are that portion of the products of such labor which the power of the master enables him to appropriate. These profits are less, because the master allows the slave to retain a larger share of the results of his own labor, than do the employers of free labor. But we not only boast that the White Slave Trade is more exacting and fraudulent (in fact, though not in intention,) than Black Slavery; but we also boast, that it is more cruel, in leaving the laborer to take care of himself and family out of the pittance which skill or capital have allowed him to retain. When the day's labor is ended, he is free, but is overburdened with the cares of family and household, which make his freedom an empty and delusive mockery. But his employer is really free, and may enjoy the profits made by others' labor, without a care, or a trouble, as to their well-being. The negro slave is free, too, when the labors of the day are over, and free in mind as well as body; for the master provides food, raiment, house, fuel, and everything else necessary to the physical well-being of himself and family. The master's labors commence just when the slave's end. No wonder men should prefer white slavery to capital, to negro slavery, since it is more profitable, and is free from all the cares and labors of black slave–holding.

Now, reader, if you wish to know yourself—to "descant on your own deformity"—read on. But if you would cherish self-conceit, self-esteem, or self-appreciation, throw down our book; for we will dispel illusions which have promoted your happiness, and shew you that what you have considered and practiced as virtue, is little better than moral Cannibalism. But you will find yourself in numerous and respectable company; for all good and respectable people are "Cannibals all," who do not labor, or who are successfully trying to live without labor, on the unrequited labor of other people:—Whilst low, bad, and disreputable people, are those who labor to support themselves, and to support said respectable people besides. . . .

But, reader, we do not wish to fire into the flock. "Thou art the man!" You are a Cannibal! and if a successful one, pride yourself on the number of your victims, quite as much as any Feejee chieftain, who breakfasts, dines and sups on human flesh.—And your conscience smites you, if you have failed to succeed, quite as much as his, when he returns from an unsuccessful foray. Probably, you are a lawyer, or a merchant, or a doctor, who have made by your business fifty thousand dollars, and retired to live on your capital. But, mark! not to spend your capital. That would be vulgar, disreputable, criminal. . . . The respectable way of living is, to make other people work for you, and to pay them nothing for so doing—and to have no concern about them after their work is done. Hence, white slave-holding is much more respectable than negro slavery—for the master works nearly as hard for the negro, as he for the master. . . . Capital commands labor, as the master does the slave. Neither pays for labor; but the master permits the slave to retain a larger allowance from the proceeds of his own labor, and hence "free labor is cheaper than slave labor." You, with the command over labor which your capital gives you, are a slave owner—a master, without the obligations of a master. They who work for you, who create your income, are slaves, without the rights of slaves. Slaves without a master! Whilst you were engaged in amassing your capital, in seeking to become independent, you were in the White Slave Trade. To become independent, is to be able to make other people support you, without being obliged to labor for them. Now, what man in society is not seeking to attain this situation? He who attains it, is a slave owner, in the worst sense. He who is in pursuit of it, is engaged in the slave trade. . . .

The negro slaves of the South are the happiest, and, in some sense, the freest people in the world. The children and the aged and infirm work not at all, and yet have all the comforts and necessaries of life provided for them. They enjoy liberty, because they are oppressed neither by care nor labor. The women do little hard work, and are protected from the despotism of their husbands by their masters. The negro men and stout boys work, on the average, in good weather, not more than nine hours a day. The balance of their time is spent in perfect abandon. Besides, they have their Sabbaths and holidays. White men, with so much of license and liberty, would die of ennui; but negroes luxuriate in corporeal and mental repose. With their faces upturned to the sun, they can sleep at any hour; and quiet sleep is the greatest of human enjoyments. "Blessed be the man who invented sleep." 'Tis happiness in itself—and results from contentment with the present, and confident assurance of the future. We do not know whether free laborers ever sleep. They are fools to do so; for, whilst they sleep, the wily and watchful capitalist is devising means to ensnare and exploit them. The free laborer must work or starve. He is more of a slave than the negro, because he works longer and harder for less allowance than the slave, and has no holiday, because the cares of life with him begin when its labors end. He has no liberty, and not a single right.

Free laborers have not a thousandth part of the rights and liberties of negro slaves. Indeed, they have not a single right or a single liberty, unless it be the right or liberty to die. But the reader may think that he and other capitalists and employers are freer than negro slaves. Your capital would soon vanish, if you dared indulge in the liberty and abandon of negroes. You hold your wealth and position by the tenure of constant watchfulness, care and circumspection. You never labor; but you are never free. . . .

"Property in man" is what all are struggling to obtain. Why should they not be obliged to take care of man, their property, as they do of their horses and their hounds, their cattle and their sheep. Now, under the delusive name of liberty, you work him, "from morn to dewy eve"— from infancy to old age—then turn him out to starve. You treat your horses and hounds better. Capital is a cruel master. The free slave trade, the commonest, yet the cruelest of trades.

Name: _____ Date: _____

Document Analysis Worksheet

1. Date/Author of Document/Author's Position: Intended Audience:

2. Why was this document written? List three points the author made that you find important.

3. List two things the document tells you about life in the United States at the time it was written.

4. Write a question to the author that the document left unanswered.

Name: _____ Date: _____

Comparative Analysis Worksheet

Choose two documents from this week's readings in which the document authors present different takes on a particular issue.

1. Identify two or three key points on which the authors agree and/or disagree.

_____

_____

_____

_____

_____

_____

_____

2. Develop your analysis of these two documents further by answering one or two questions listed in the "Questions to Consider" section for each document.

_____

_____

_____

_____

_____

_____

_____

_____

_____

_____

_____

William H. Seward Calls for Support of the New Republican Party

Context: *William H. Seward was a Whig politician from New York who became one of the leaders of the new Republican Party. Seward was favored to become the Republican nominee for president in 1860, but he lost the nomination to Abraham Lincoln because some Republicans feared he was too radical on the slavery issue. Seward would later become Lincoln's Secretary of State. This speech, given in the aftermath of the Kansas-Nebraska controversy, was designed to attract antislavery Whigs and Democrats to the fledging Republican Party.*

Questions to Consider: *What evidence did Seward present to bolster his claim that slaveholders were a threat to the political liberty of northerners? Why did Seward invoke the Declaration of Independence and American Revolution? How did Seward counter the argument that slavery was protected by the Constitution? Did Seward show any sympathy for the slaves themselves?*

William H. Seward, The Dangers of Extending Slavery, and the Contest and the Crisis. Delivered in Albany, October 12, 1855

The nation was founded on the simple and practically new principle of the equal and inalienable rights of all men, and therefore it necessarily became a republic. Other Governments, founded on the ancient principle of the inequality of men, are, by force of an equal necessity, monarchies or aristocracies. Whenever either of these kinds of Government loses by lapse of time and change of circumstances its elementary principle, whether of equality or inequality, thenceforward it takes a rapid and irresistible course toward a reorganization of the opposite kind. No one, here or elsewhere, is so disloyal to his country or to mankind as to be willing to see our republican system fail. All agree that in every case, and throughout all hazards, aristocracy must be abhorred and avoided, and republican institutions must be defended and preserved.

Think it not strange or extravagant when I say that an aristocracy has already arisen here, and that it is already undermining the Republic. An aristocracy could not arise in any country where there was no privileged class, and no special foundation on which such a class could permanently stand. On the contrary, every State, however republican its Constitution may be, is sure to become an aristocracy, sooner or later, if it has a privileged class standing firmly on an enduring special foundation; and if that class is continually growing stronger and stronger, and the unprivileged classes are continually growing weaker and weaker. It is not at all essential to a privileged class that it rest on feudal tenures, or on military command, or on ecclesiastical authority, or that its rights be hereditary, or even that it be distinguished by titles of honor. It may be even the more insidious and more dangerous for lacking all these things, because it will be less obnoxious to popular hostility.

A privileged class has existed in this country, from an early period of its settlement. Slave-holders constitute that class. They have a special foundation on which to stand—namely, personal dominion over slaves. Conscience and sound policy forbid all men alike from holding slaves, but some citizens disregard the injunction. Some of the States enforce the inhibition; other States neglect or refuse to enforce it. In all of the States, there are but three hundred and fifty thousand citizens who avail themselves of this peculiar indulgence; and those, protected by the laws of their States, constitute a privileged class. They confess themselves to be such a class, when they designate the system of Slavery as a "peculiar" institution.

The spirit of the revolutionary age was adverse to that privileged class. America and Europe were firmly engaged then in prosecuting what was expected to be a speedy, complete, and universal abolition of African Slavery. Nearly all of the privileged class admitted that Slavery as a permanent system was indefensible, and favored its removal. They asked only, what seemed by no means unreasonable, some securities against a sudden, rash, and violent removal of the evil. Under these circumstances, even the most decided opponents of Slavery consented to some provisions of the Federal Constitution which were inconsistent with the stern logic of equality that pervaded all its other parts, and pervaded the whole of the Declaration of American Independence, on which the Constitution itself was based. We are not to censure the fathers for these concessions; they had a union of the States to create, and to their ardent and generous minds the voluntary removal of Slavery, by the action of the several States themselves, without Federal interference, seemed not only certain, but close at hand.

These provisions of the Constitution were:

First: That the foreign slave trade should not be abolished before 1808.

Second: That any law or regulation which any State might establish in favor of Freedom, should not impair the legal remedy, then supposed to exist by common law, for the recapture, by legal process, in such State, of fugitives from labor or service, escaping from other States.

Third: That three-fifths of all slaves should be counted, in settling the basis of representation in the several States.

These three concessions, which in themselves seem very limited, and almost harmless are all that the fathers consciously made to the privileged class.

But privileged classes always know well how to improve even any indirect advantages which the Constitution or laws of a country afford. Such indirect advantages they acquired from two other provisions of the Constitution: 1st. That provision which makes the State authority independent and sovereign in municipal affairs, Slavery being understood to be purely municipal in its nature. 2nd. That provision which, out of tenderness to the small States, gives them a representation in the Senate equal to that of the largest State. . . .

Thus we see that the American slaveholders are a privileged class, standing on a special and permanent foundation, and that they are protected in their advantages by the organic laws.

A privileged class, thus established on an exceptional principle that is wrong in itself, and antagonistic to the fundamental principle of the Government, must necessarily be dangerous, if it be suffered to expand and aggrandize itself. . . . The invention of the cotton gin, which easily separates the seed from the fibre, has made cotton an almost exclusive agricultural staple in the States of the privileged class, and an eminent commercial staple of the whole country. The national territory has necessarily been enlarged, from time to time, to accommodate an overgrowing population and an ever-increasing commerce. Favored by these circumstances, the privileged class have at the same time found, in a home production of slaves in Maryland and Virginia and other States, a compensation for the loss of the African slave trade; and they have not been slothful in unlearning all the fears and dismissing all the timidity and conciliation which marked their conduct during and immediately after the revolutionary war.

. . . [In the 1830s] The privileged class . . . entered Texas, established Slavery there in violation of Mexican laws, detached that territory from Mexico, and organized it as an independent sovereign State. Texas, thus independent and sovereign, sought annexation to the United States. . . . A war [with Mexico] ensued, and terminated in the transfer of the northern portion of Mexico to the United States. . . . [T]he privileged class demand either an equal partition, or that the whole should be opened to their colonization with slaves. The House of Representatives resisted these pretensions, as it had resisted similar ones before; but the Senate seconded the privileged class with its accustomed zeal. So Congress was divided, and failed to organize civil Governments for the newly acquired Mexican territories, and they were left under martial law.

You all know well the way of that memorable controversy. . . How the Missouri Compromise, which extended that Ordinance across the Mississippi, and over all Kansas and Nebraska, was made at once the authority, precedent, and formula, of the new compromise, and even declared to be an irrepealable law forever. How California, which refused to become a slave State, was admitted into the Union as a free one. How the hateful and detestable slave auctions were banished from under the eaves of the Capitol, quite across to the opposite banks of the Potomac River. And how, in consideration of these magnanimous and vast concessions made by the privileged class, it was stipulated that Slavery should be continued in the District of Columbia as long as the privileged class should require its continuance. . . .

You remember how it was solemnly stipulated that Utah and New Mexico, if the slaveholders could corrupt them, should come into the Union, in due time, as slaveholding States; and, finally, how the privileged class, so highly offended and exasperated, were brought to accept this compromise on their part, by a re-enactment of the then obsolete fugitive slave law of 1793, with the addition of the revolting features of an attempted suspension of the habeas corpus; an absolute prohibition of the trial by jury; and effective repeal of vital rules of procedure and evidence, and the substitution of commissioners in place of courts of justice, in derogation of the Constitution. . . .

Nevertheless, scarcely one year had elapsed, before the privileged class, using some of our own representatives as their instruments, broke up not only this Compromise of 1850, but even the Compromise of 1820 and the Ordinance of 1787, and obtained the declaration of Congress, that all these settlements, so far as they were adverse to the privileged class, were unconstitutional usurpations of legislative power.

I do not dwell, as others so often and so justly do, upon the atrocious usurpation of the government of Kansas by the slaveholders of Missouri, nor even on the barbarous and tyrannical code which they have established to stifle Freedom in that Territory. . . You are commanded by an unconstitutional law of Congress to seize and deliver up to the members of that privileged class their fugitive slaves, under pain of imprisonment and forfeiture of your estates. You may not interpose between the armed slaveholder and the wounded slave, to prevent his being murdered, without coming under arrest for treason, nor may you cover his naked and lacerated limbs except by stealth. You may not tell the freed slave who reaches your borders that he is free, without being seized by a Federal Court, and condemned, without a trial or even an accusation, to an imprisonment without bail. . . . The President of the United States is reduced to the position of a deputy of the privileged class, emptying the treasury and marshalling battalions and ships of war to dragoon you into the execution of the Fugitive Slave Law on the one hand, while he removes Governors and Judges, at their command, who attempt to maintain lawful and constitutional resistance against them in the Territory of Kansas. . . .

The change, that has become at last so necessary, is as easy to be made as it is necessary. The whole number of slaveholders is only three hundred and fifty thousand, one-hundredth part of the entire population of the country. If you add their parents, children, immediate relatives and dependents, they are two millions—one-fifteenth part of the American people. Slavery is not, and never can be, perpetual. It will be overthrown either peacefully or lawfully under this Constitution, or it will work the subversion of the Constitution, together with its own overthrow. Then the slaveholders would perish in the struggle. The change can now be made without violence, and by the agency of the ballot-box. . . .

The will exists, because the evil has become intolerable, and the need of a remedy is universally acknowledged. What, then, is wanted? Organization. Organization! . . .

We must restore the demoralized virtue of the nation. We must restore the principle of equality among the members of the State—the principle of the sacredness of the absolute and inherent rights of man. We want, then, an organization open to all classes of men, and that excludes none. . . .

The Republican organization has sagaciously seen this, and magnanimously laid a new, sound, and liberal platform. . . . Its principles are equal and exact justice; its speech open, decided, and frank. Its banner is untorn in former battles, and unsullied by past errors. That is the party for us. I do not know that it will always, or even long, preserve its courage, its moderation, and its consistency. If it shall do so, it will rescue and save the country. If it, too, shall become unfaithful, as all preceding parties have done, it will, without sorrow or regret on my part, perish as they are perishing, and will give place to another truer and better one. . . .

Document Ten

Hinton Rowan Helper Attacks Slavery

Context: *Hinton Rowan Helper was a small farmer from western North Carolina, a region of the South that had very few slaves. His economic critique of the South reflected the sentiments of northern free labor ideology. Helper's book—*The Impending Crisis *(1857)—was banned in some southern states, but was extremely popular in the North. The Republican Party published an abridged edition that many congressmen endorsed.*

Questions to Consider: *What is the basis for Helper's critique of the slavery? Why did Helper include so many statistics in his argument? How does his antislavery appeal differ from the rhetoric of northern abolitionists? Does Helper show sympathy for the slaves themselves? Why did southern slaveholders find Helper's arguments particularly dangerous?*

Selection from Hinton Rowan Helper, *The Impending Crisis* (1857)

Comparisons are at the bottom of all philosophy. It is by comparisons that we ascertain the difference which exists between things, and it is by comparisons, also, that we ascertain the general features of things, and it is by comparisons that we reach general propositions. Without comparisons we never can generalize. Without comparisons we never could go beyond the knowledge of isolated, disconnected facts. . . .

New York and Virginia

In 1790, when the first census was taken, New York contained 340,120 inhabitants; at the same time the population of Virginia was 748,308, being more than twice the number of New York. Just sixty years afterward, as we learn from the census of 1850, New York had a population of 3,097,394; while that of Virginia was only 1,421,661, being less than half the number of New York! In 1791, the exports of New York amounted to $2,505,465; the exports of Virginia amounted to $3,130,865. In 1852, the exports of New York amounted to $87,484,456; the exports of Virginia, during the same year, amounted to only $2,724,657. In 1790, the imports of New York and Virginia were about equal; in 1853, the imports of New York amounted to the enormous sum of $178,270,999: while those of Virginia, for the same period, amounted to the comparatively pitiful aggregate of only $399,004. In 1850, the products of manufactures, mining and the mechanics arts in New York amounted to $237,597,249; those of Virginia amounted to only $29,705,387. At the taking of the last census, the value of real and personal property in Virginia, including Negroes, was $391,646,438; that of New York, exclusive of any monetary valuation of human beings, was $1,080,309,216. In August, 1856, the real and personal estate assessed in the City of New York amounted in valuation to $511,740,491, showing that New York City alone is worth far more than the whole State of Virginia. . . .

The cash value of all the farms, farming implements and machinery in Virginia, in 1850, was $223,423,315; the value of the same in New York, in the same year, was $576,631,568. . . . But we will pursue this humiliating comparison no further. With feelings mingled with indignation and disgust, we turn from the picture, and will now pay our respects to

Massachusetts and North Carolina

In 1790, Massachusetts contained 378,717 inhabitants; in the same year North Carolina contained 393,751; in 1850, the population of Massachusetts was 994,514, all freemen; while that of North Carolina was only 869,039, of whom 288,548 were slaves. Massachusetts has an area of only 7,800 square miles; the area of North Carolina is 50,704 square miles, which, though less than Virginia, is considerably larger than the State of New York. Massachusetts and North Carolina each have a harbor, Boston and Beaufort, which harbors, with the States that back them, are, by nature, possessed of about equal capacities and advantages for commercial and manufacturing enterprise. Boston has grown to be the second commercial city in the Union; her ships, freighted with the useful and unique inventions and manufactures of her ingenious artisans and mechanics, and bearing upon their stalwart arms the majestic flag of our country, glide triumphantly through the winds and over the waves of every ocean. She has done, and is now doing, great honor to herself, her State and the nation, and her name and fame are spoken with reverence in the remotest regions of the earth. How is it with Beaufort, in North Carolina, whose harbor is said to be the safest and most commodious anywhere to be found on the Atlantic coast south of the harbor of New York, and but little inferior to that? Has anybody ever heard of her? . . . But we will make no further attempt to draw a comparison between the populous, wealthy, and renowned city of Boston and the obscure, despicable little village of Beaufort, which, notwithstanding "thee placid bosom of its deep and well-protected harbor," has no place in the annals or records of the country, and has scarcely ever been hear fifty miles from home?! . . .

Pennsylvania and South Carolina

An old gentleman, now residing in Charleston, told us, but a short while ago, that he had a distinct recollection of the time when Charleston imported foreign fabrics for the Philadelphia trade, and when, on a certain occasion, his mother went into a store on Market street to select a silk dress for herself, the merchant, unable to please her fancy, persuaded her to postpone the selection for a few days, or until the arrival of a new stock of superb styles and fashions which he had recently purchased in the metropolis of South Carolina.

. . . A most unfortunate day was that for the Palmetto State, and indeed for the whole South, when the course of trade was changed, and she found herself the retailer of foreign and domestic goods, imported and vended by wholesale merchants at the North. Philadelphia ladies no longer look to the South for late fashions, and fine silks and satins; no Quaker dame now wears drab apparel of Charleston importation. Like all other centres of trade in our disreputable part of the confederacy, the commercial emporium of South Carolina is sick and impoverished; her silver cord has been loosed; her golden bowl has been broken; and her unhappy people, without proper or profitable employment, poor in pocket, and few in number, go mourning or loafing about the streets. Her annual importations are actually less now than they were a century ago, when South Carolina was the second commercial province on the continent, Virginia being the first. . . .

In Pennsylvania, in 1850, the annual income of public schools amounted to $1,348,249; the same in South Carolina, in the same year, amounted to only $200,600; in the former State there were 393 libraries other than private, in the latter only 26; in Pennsylvania 310 newspapers and periodicals were published, circulating 84,898,672 copies annually; in South Carolina only 46 newspapers and periodicals were published, circulating but 7,145,930 copies per annum.

The incontrovertible facts we have thus far presented are, we think, amply sufficient, both in number and magnitude, to bring conviction to the mind of every candid reader, that there is something wrong, socially, politically and morally wrong, in the policy under which the South has so long loitered and languished. Else, how is it that the North, under the operations of a policy directly the opposite of ours, has surpassed us in almost everything great and good, and left us standing before the world, an object of merited reprehension and derision? For one, we are heartily ashamed of the inexcusable weakness, inertia and dilapidation everywhere so manifest throughout our native section; but the blame properly attaches itself to an usurping minority of the people, and we are determined that it shall rest where it belongs. More on this subject, however, after a brief but general survey of the inequalities and disparities that exist between those two grand divisions of the country.

Why the North has Surpassed the South

And now that we have come to the very heart and soul of our subject, we feel no disposition to mince matters, but mean to speak plainly and to the point, without any equivocation, mental reservation, or secret evasion whatever. The son of a venerated parent, who, while he lived, was a considerate and merciful slaveholder, a native of the South, born and bred in North Carolina, of a family whose home has been in the valley of the Yadkin for nearly a century and a Southerner by instinct and by all the influences of thought, habits and kindred, and with the desire and fixed purpose to reside permanently within the limits of the South, and with the expectation of dying there also-we feel that we have the right to express our opinion, however humble or unimportant it may be, on any and every question that affects the public good; and, so help us God, "sink or swim, live or die, survive or perish," we are determined to exercise that right with manly firmness, and without fear, favor or affection. And now to the point. In our opinion, an opinion which has been formed from data obtained by assiduous researches, and comparisons, from laborious investigation, logical reasoning, and earnest reflection, the causes which have impeded the progress and prosperity of the South, which have dwindled our commerce and other similar pursuits, into the most contemptible insignificance; sunk a large majority of our people in galling poverty and ignorance, rendered a small minority conceited and tyrannical, and driven the rest away from their homes; entailed upon us a humiliating dependence on the Free States; disgraced us in the recesses of our own souls and brought us under reproach in the eyes of all civilized and enlightened nations—may all be traced to one common source, and there find solution in the most hateful and horrible word, that was ever incorporated into the vocabulary of human economy—Slavery.

Reared amidst the institution of slavery, believing it to be wrong both in principle and in practice, and having seen and felt its evil influences upon individuals, communities and states, we deem it a duty, no less than a privilege, to enter our protest against it, and, as a Southern man, to use all constitutional means and our most strenuous efforts to overturn and abolish it. Our repugnance to slavery springs from no one-sided idea, or sickly sentimentality. We have not been hasty in making up our mind on the subject; we have jumped at no conclusions; we have acted with perfect calmness and deliberation; we have carefully considered, and examined the reasons for and against the institution, and have also taken into account the probable consequences of our decision. . . .

Though neither a prophet nor the son of a prophet, our vision is sufficiently penetrative to divine the future so far as to be able to see that the "peculiar institution" has but a short and, as heretofore, inglorious existence before it. Time, the righter of every wrong, is ripening events for the desired consummation of our labors and the fulfillment of our cherished hopes. Each revolving year brings nearer the inevitable crisis. The sooner it comes the better; may heaven, through our humble efforts, hasten its advent. The first and most sacred duty of every Southerner, who has the honor and the interest of his country at heart, is to declare himself an unqualified and uncompromising opponent of slavery. No conditional or half-way declaration will avail; no mere threatening demonstration will succeed. With those who desire to be instrumental in bringing about the triumph of liberty over slavery, there should be neither evasion, vacillation, nor equivocation. We should listen to no modifying terms or compromises that may be proposed by the proprietors of the unprofitable and ungodly institution. Nothing short of the complete abolition of slavery can save the South from falling into the vortex of utter ruin. Too long have we yielded a submissive obedience to the tyrannical domination of an inflated oligarchy; too long have we tolerated their arrogance and self-conceit; too long have we submitted to their unjust and savage exactions. Let us now wrest from them the sceptre of power, establish liberty and equal rights throughout the land, and henceforth and forever guard our legislative halls from the pollutions and usurpations of pro-slavery demagogues.

Document Eleven

Republicans Adopt Anti-Slavery Platform

Context: *When the Republican Party met in 1860, it faced the difficult task of satisfying its abolitionist wing while avoiding positions that would alienate more conservative voters. The resulting platform attempted to walk that fine line. Supporting this platform, Republican nominee Abraham Lincoln carried every northern state, except New Jersey.*

Questions to Consider: *Did the Republicans endorse either the abolition of slavery or repeal of the Fugitive Slave Act? Can you locate the veiled references to the Dred Scott Case and John Brown's Raid? What was ultimately more important to the Republican Party: economic issues such as the tariff and internal improvements, or the questions surrounding the expansion of slavery?*

Republican National Platform, Adopted at Chicago, 1860

Resolved, That we, the delegated representatives of the Republican electors of the United States, in Convention assembled, in discharge of the duty we owe to our constituents and our country, unite in the following declarations:

That the history of the nation, during the last four years, has fully established the propriety and necessity of the organization and perpetuation of the Republican party, and that the causes which called it into existence are permanent in their nature, and now, more than ever before, demand its peaceful and constitutional triumph.

That the maintenance of the principles promulgated in the Declaration of Independence and embodied in the Federal Constitution, "That all men are created equal; that they are endowed by their Creator with certain inalienable rights; that among these are life, liberty, and the pursuit of happiness; that to secure these rights, governments are instituted among men, deriving their just powers from the consent of the governed," is essential to the preservation of our Republican institutions; and that the Federal Constitution, the Rights of the States, and the Union of the States, must and shall be preserved.

That to the Union of the States this nation owes its unprecedented increase in population, its surprising development of material resources, its rapid augmentation of wealth, its happiness at home and its honor abroad; and we hold in abhorrence all schemes for Disunion, come from whatever source they may: And we congratulate the country that no Republican member of Congress has uttered or countenanced the threats of Disunion so often made by Democratic members without rebuke and with applause from their political associates; and we denounce those threats of Disunion, in case of a popular overthrow of their ascendancy, as denying the vital principles of a free government, and as an avowal of contemplated treason, which it is the imperative duty of an indignant People sternly to rebuke and forever silence.

That the maintenance inviolate of the rights of the States, and especially the right of each State to order and control its own domestic institutions according to its own judgment exclusively, is essential to that balance of powers on which the perfection and endurance of our political fabric depends; and we denounce the lawless invasion by armed force of the soil of any State or Territory, no matter under what pretext, as among the gravest of crimes.

That the present Democratic Administration has far exceeded our worst apprehensions, in its measureless subservience to the exactions of a sectional interest, as especially evinced in its desperate exertions to force the infamous Lecompton Constitution upon the protesting people of Kansas; in construing the personal relation between master and servant to involve an unqualified property in persons; in its attempted enforcement, everywhere, on land and sea, through the intervention of Congress and of the Federal Courts of the extreme pretensions of a purely local interest; and in its general and unvarying abuse of the power entrusted to it by a confiding people.

That the people justly view with alarm the reckless extravagance which pervades every department of the Federal Government; that a return to rigid economy and accountability is indispensable to arrest the systematic plunder of the public treasury by favored partisans, while the recent startling developments of frauds and corruptions at the Federal metropolis, show that an entire change of administration is imperatively demanded.

That the new dogma, that the Constitution, of its own force, carries Slavery into any or all of the Territories of the United States, is a dangerous political heresy, at variance with the explicit provisions of that instrument itself, with contemporaneous exposition, and with legislative and judicial precedent; is revolutionary in its tendency, and subversive of the peace and harmony of the country. . . .

That in the recent vetoes, by their Federal Governors, of the acts of the Legislatures of Kansas and Nebraska, prohibiting Slavery in those Territories, we find a practical illustration of the boasted Democratic principle of Non-Intervention and Popular Sovereignty, embodied in the Kansas-Nebraska bill, and a demonstration of the deception and fraud involved therein.

That Kansas should, of right, be immediately admitted as a State under the Constitution recently formed and adopted by her people, and accepted by the House of Representatives.

That, while providing revenue for the support of the General Government by duties upon imports, sound policy requires such an adjustment of these imposts as to encourage the development of the industrial interest of the whole country; and we commend that policy of national exchanges which secures to the working men liberal wages, to agriculture remunerative prices, to mechanics and manufactures an adequate reward for their skill, labor, and enterprise, and to the nation commercial prosperity and independence.

That we protest against any sale or alienation to others of the Public Lands held by actual settlers, and against any view of the Homestead policy which regards the settlers as paupers or suppliants for public bounty; and we demand the passage by Congress of the complete and satisfactory Homestead measure which has already passed the House. . . .

That appropriations by Congress for River and Harbor improvements of a National character, required for the accommodation and security of an existing commerce, are authorized by the Constitution, and justified by the obligations of Government to protect the lives and property of its citizens.

That a Railroad to the Pacific Ocean is imperatively demanded by the interest of the whole country; that the Federal Government ought to render immediate and efficient aid in its construction; and that, as preliminary thereto, a daily Overland Mail should be promptly established. . . .

Document Twelve

South Carolinians Justify Secession

Context: *With the election of Abraham Lincoln in November of 1860, South Carolinians moved quickly to leave the Union. The secession movement had overwhelming support in South Carolina, which had traditionally been the most radical of the southern states. This address solicited the support of other southern states. By February of 1861, all of the "cotton" states (South Carolina, Georgia, Florida, Alabama, Mississippi, Louisiana, and Texas) had left the Union.*

Questions to Consider: *What parallels did South Carolinians draw between the American Revolution and their own cause? What view of democracy is embedded in this address? In what ways did this document highlight the profound mistrust between northerners and southerners?*

"The Address of the People of South Carolina, Assembled in Convention, to the People of the Slaveholding States of the United States." (December 1860)

It is seventy-three years since the Union between the United States was made by the Constitution of the United States. During this time, their advance in wealth, prosperity and power has been with scarcely a parallel in the history of the world. The great object of their Union was defense against external aggression of more powerful nations; which object is now attained, from their mere progress in power. Thirty-one millions of people, with a commerce and navigation which explore every sea, and with agricultural productions which are necessary to every civilized people, command the friendship of the world. But unfortunately, our internal peace has not grown with our external prosperity. Discontent and contention have moved in the bosom of the Confederacy for the last thirty-five years. . . .

The one great evil, from which all other evils have flowed, is the overthrow of the Constitution of the United States. The Government of the United States is no longer the Government of Confederated Republics, but of a consolidated Democracy. It is no longer a free government, but a Despotism. It is, in fact, such a Government as Great Britain attempted to set over our fathers; and which was resisted and defeated by a seven years' struggle for independence.

The Revolution of 1776 turned upon one great principle of self-government and self-taxation; the criterion of self-government. Where the interests of two people united together under one Government, are different, each must have the power to protect its interests by the organization of the Government, or they cannot be free. The interests of Great Britain and of the Colonies were different and antagonistic. Great Britain was desirous of carrying out the policy of all nations towards their Colonies, of making them tributary to her wealth and power. She had vast and complicated relations with the whole world. Her policy towards her North American Colonies was to identify them with her in all these complicated relations; and to make them bear, in common with the rest of the Empire, the full burden of her obligations and necessities. . . . To make them a part of a consolidated Empire, the Parliament of Great Britain determined to assume the power of legislating for the Colonies in all cases whatsoever. Our ancestors resisted the pretension. They refused to be a part of the consolidated Government of Great Britain.

The Southern States now stand exactly in the same position towards the Northern States that the Colonies did towards Great Britain. The Northern States, having the majority in Congress, claim the same power of omnipotence in legislation as the British Parliament. "The General Welfare," is the only limit to the legislation of either; and the majority in Congress, as in the British Parliament, are the sole judges of the expediency of the legislation this "General Welfare" requires. Thus, the Government of the United States has become a consolidated Government; and the people of the Southern States are compelled to meet the very despotism their fathers threw off in the Revolution of 1776.

The consolidation of the Government of Great Britain over the Colonies, was attempted to be carried out by the taxes. The British Parliament undertook to tax the Colonies, to promote British interests. Our fathers resisted this pretension. They claimed the right of self-taxation through their Colonial Legislatures. They were not represented in the British Parliament, and, therefore, could not rightly be taxed by its Legislation. . . . Hence, they refused to pay the taxes laid by the British Parliament.

And so with the Southern States, towards the Northern States, in the vital matter of taxation. They are in a minority in Congress. Their representation in Congress is useless to protect them against unjust taxation; and they are taxed by the people of the North for their benefit, exactly as the people of Great Britain taxed our ancestors in the British Parliament for their benefit. . . . The people of the South have been taxed by duties on imports, not for revenue, but for an object inconsistent with revenue—to promote, by prohibitions, Northern interests in the productions of their mines and manufactures. . . .

The people of the Southern States are not only taxed for the benefit of the Northern States, but after the taxes are collected, three-fourths of them are expended at the North. This cause, with others, connected with the operation of the General Government, has made the cities of the South provincial. Their growth is paralyzed; they are mere suburbs of Northern cities.

The agricultural productions of the South are the basis of the foreign commerce of the United States; yet Southern cities do not carry it on. Our foreign trade is almost annihilated.

No man can, for a moment, believe that our ancestors intended to establish over their posterity, exactly the same sort of Government they had overthrown. The great object of the Constitution of the United States, in its internal operation, was, doubtless, to secure the great end of the Revolution—a limited free Government—a Government limited to those matters only, which were general and common to all portions of the United States. All sectional or local interests were to be left to the States. By no other arrangement would they obtain free Government, by a Constitution common to so vast a Confederacy. Yet, by gradual and steady encroachments on the part of the people of the North, and acquiescence on the part of the South, the limitations in the Constitution have been swept away; and the Government of the United States has become consolidated, with a claim of limitless powers in its operations.

It is not at all surprising, whilst such is the character of the Government of the United States, that it should assume to possess power over all the institutions of the country. The agitations on the subject of slavery are the natural results of the consolidation of the Government. Responsibility follows power; and if the people of the North have the power by Congress "to promote the general welfare of the United States," by any means they deem expedient—why should they not assail and overthrow the institution of slavery in the South? They are responsible for its continuance or existence, in proportion to their power. A majority in Congress, according to their interested and perverted views, is omnipotent. . . .

The Constitution of the United States was an experiment. The experiment consisted in uniting under one Government, different peoples living in different climates, and having different pursuits of industry and institutions. It matters not how carefully the limitations of such a Government be laid down in the Constitution—its success must, at least, depend upon the good faith of the parties to the constitutional compact, in enforcing them. . . . The experiment has been fairly made. The Southern States, from the commencement of the Government, have striven to keep it within the orbit prescribed by the Constitution. The experiment has failed. The whole Constitution, by the constructions of the Northern people, has been absorbed by its preamble. . . . [t]he General Government [thus] must necessarily be a despotism, because all sectional or local interests must ever be represented by a minority in the councils of the General Government, having no power to protect itself against the rule of the majority. The majority, constituted from those who do not represent these sectional or local interests, will control and govern them. A free people cannot submit to such a Government. . . .

Under such a Government, there must, of course, be many and endless "irrepressible conflicts," between the two great sections of the Union. The same faithlessness which has abolished the Constitution of the United States, will not fail to carry out the sectional purposes for which it has been abolished. There must be conflict; and the weaker section of the Union can only find peace and liberty in an independence of the North. . . . It is now too late to reform or restore the Government of the United States. All confidence in the North is lost by the South. The faithlessness of the North for half a century has opened a gulf of separation between the North and the South which no promises nor engagements can fill. . . .

The Union of the Constitution was a Union of slaveholding States. It rests on slavery, by prescribing a representation in Congress for three-fifths of our slaves. . . . Time and the progress of things have totally altered the relations between the Northern and Southern States, since the Union was established. That identity of feelings, interests and institutions which once existed, is gone. They are now divided, between agricultural and manufacturing, and commercial States; between slaveholding and non-slaveholding States. Their institutions and industrial pursuits have made them totally different peoples. That equality in the Government between the two sections of the Union which once existed, no longer exists. We but imitate the policy of our fathers in dissolving a union with non-slaveholding confederates, and seeking a confederation with slaveholding States.

Experience has proved that slaveholding States cannot be safe in subjection to non-slaveholding States. Indeed, no people can ever expect to preserve its rights and liberties, unless these be in its own custody. To plunder and oppress, where plunder and oppression can be practiced with impunity, seems to be the natural order of things. The fairest portions of the world elsewhere, have been turned into wildernesses, and the most civilized and prosperous communities have been impoverished and ruined by anti-slavery fanaticism. The people of the North have not left us in doubt as to their designs and policy. United as a section in the late Presidential election, they have elected as the exponent of their policy, one who has openly declared that all the States of the United States must be made free States or slave States. It is true, that amongst those who aided in his election, there are various shades of anti-slavery hostility. But if African slavery in the Southern States be the evil their political combination affirms it to be, the requisitions of an inexorable logic must lead them to emancipation. If it is right to preclude or abolish slavery in a Territory, why should it be allowed to remain in the States? The one is not at all more unconstitutional than the other, according to the decisions of the Supreme Court of the United States. And when it is considered that the Northern States will soon have the power to make that Court what they please, and that the Constitution never has been any barrier whatever to their exercise of power, what check can there be, in the unrestrained counsels of the North, to emancipation? . . . The hypocrisy of thirty years—the faithlessness of their whole course from the commencement of our union with them, show that the people of the non-slaveholding North are not, and cannot be safe associates of the slaveholding South, under a common Government. . . .

South Carolina, acting in her sovereign capacity, now thinks proper to secede from the Union. She did not part with her Sovereignty in adopting the Constitution. The last thing a State can be presumed to have surrendered, is her Sovereignty. Her Sovereignty is her life. Nothing but a clear express grant can alienate it. Inference has no place. Yet it is not at all surprising that those who have construed away all the limitations of the Constitution, should also by construction, claim the annihilation of the Sovereignty of the States. . . . The truth is, they having violated the express provisions of the Constitution, it is at an end, as a compact. It is morally obligatory only on those who choose to accept its perverted terms. South Carolina, deeming the compact not only violated in particular features, but virtually abolished by her Northern confederates, withdraws herself as a party from its obligations. The right to do so is denied by her Northern confederates. They desire to establish a sectional despotism, not only omnipotent in Congress, but omnipotent over the States; and as if to manifest the imperious necessity of our secession, they threaten us with the sword, to coerce submission to their rule.

Citizens of the slaveholding States of the United States! Circumstances beyond our control have placed us in the van of the great controversy between the Northern and Southern States. . . . Providence has cast our lot together, by extending over us an identity of pursuits, interests, and institutions. South Carolina desires no destiny separated from yours. To be one of a great Slaveholding Confederacy, stretching its arms over a territory larger than any power in Europe possesses—with a population four times greater than that of the whole United States when they achieved their independence of the British Empire—with productions which make our existence more important to the world than that of any other people inhabiting it—with common institutions to defend, and common dangers to encounter—we ask your sympathy and confederation. . . . You have long lingered in hope over the shattered remains of a broken Constitution. Compromise after compromise, formed by your concessions, has been trampled under foot by your Northern confederates. All fraternity of feeling between the North and the South is lost, or has been converted into hate; and we, of the South, are at last driven together by the stern destiny which controls the existence of nations. . . .

If they prefer a system of industry, in which capital and labor are in perpetual conflict—and chronic starvation keeps down the natural increase of population—and a man is worked out in eight years—and the law ordains that children shall be worked only ten hours a day—and the sabre and the bayonet are the instruments of order—be it so. It is their affair, not ours. We prefer, however, our system of industry, by which labor and capital are identified in interest, and capital, therefore, protects labor—by which our population doubles every twenty years— which starvation is unknown, and abundance crowns the land—by which order is preserved by an unpaid police, and many fertile regions of the world, where the Caucasian cannot labor, are brought into usefulness by the labor of the African, and the whole world is blessed by our productions. All we demand of other peoples is to be left alone, to work out our own high destinies. United together, and we must be the most independent, as we are among the most important, of the nations of the world. United together, and we require no other instrument to conquer peace, than our beneficent productions. United together, and we must be a great, free and prosperous people, whose renown must spread throughout the civilized world, and pass down, we trust, to the remotest ages. We ask you to join us in forming a Confederacy of Slaveholding States.

Name: _____ Date: _____

Document Analysis Worksheet

1. Date/Author of Document/Author's Position: Intended Audience:

2. Why was this document written? List three points the author made that you find important.

3. List two things the document tells you about life in the United States at the time it was written.

4. Write a question to the author that the document left unanswered.

Comparative Analysis Worksheet

Choose two documents from this week's readings in which the document authors present different takes on a particular issue.

    1. Identify two or three key points on which the authors agree and/or disagree.

_____

_____

_____

_____

_____

_____

    2. Develop your analysis of these two documents further by answering one or two questions listed in the "Questions to Consider" section for each document.

_____

_____

_____

_____

_____

_____

_____

_____

_____

_____

Document Thirteen

Refugees from Slavery Flood Northern Lines

Context: *During the Civil War, tens of thousands of escaped or captured slaves headed for northern lines. These refugees presented political questions that northerners had not anticipated. What was the legal status of these escaped slaves? Should they be allowed to work for the army? Should the Union army provide them with rations and material aid? The following report, issued in December of 1862 by the Society of Friends (the Quakers), outlines the extent of the problem. The Quakers, it should be noted, were staunch abolitionists.*

Questions to Consider: *According to the report, what motivated slaves to escape to Union lines? What conditions did the ex-slaves face when in northern camps? How did the report counter proslavery ideology and why did it emphasize the refugees' desire to remain in the South? Speculate on the political impact of refugees. In what ways did they encourage Lincoln and other northern politicians to abolish slavery?*

Report of a Committee of Representatives of New York Yearly Meeting of Friends upon the Condition and Wants of the Colored Refugees. (December 1862)

Pursuant to appointment, the committee has visited . . . several thousand of the [black] refugees, of all ages and conditions. We received polite attention from all the officers of government upon whom we called, and every facility to accomplish the desired investigation.

During this engagement, we have met with much to interest us and excite our sympathy in behalf of multitudes of our fellow-men, now passing through painful vicissitudes, in their transition from a state of bondage and degradation to an unknown future, which, though enveloped in present darkness, and filled with trial and sorrow, is yet lighted by hope, and cheered and comforted by faith and trust in the wisdom and mercy of the Almighty. . . .

The present shelter of the refugees in Washington is called Camp Barker. We visited it on the 25th of 11th month. It consists of a large oblong square, surrounded on three sides by huts or barracks, and other buildings, all opening within the square; and by a high fence on the west side. The entrance is under a military guard. The huts, about forty-eight in number, are about twelve feet square, and each have from ten to twelve inmates. There are also several large tents, occupied by old or infirm men, and two buildings called hospitals—one for men, and one for women. The residence of the superintendent is within the enclosure. . . .

The superintendent reported as follows: There were 400 in camp, on the 16th of June (when he came). Since then there have come in 3,350—making a total of 3,750. Of these 280 have died. The present number is from 600 to 650, of whom 231 are children. The rest have found employment about Washington in various service—excepting about 20 who have gone North. They generally object to go there on account of the cold. There are 125 sick, all of whom have been sent in from other places, except about 25 who have sickened in the camp. This place is the general receptacle for the sick of about 6,000 refugees in and around Washington. The superintendent did not report the number of births, but they are not equal to the deaths.

The government gives employment to all the able-bodied men, at wages according to their service, from $12 to $25 per month, and all have rations except the teamsters, at the latter rate. There are about 100 women, who go out to day's work, returning at night to camp. They are said to earn fifty cents per day.

We went to Alexandria on the 26th, and called on the acting superintendent of the colored refugees there, under the Provost Marshal. He informed us there were, on the 12th of October, 1,230 refugees of all ages and conditions, quartered in twenty-five houses. We visited a considerable number of them. One had been formerly used as a slave-pen by a trader. Although the poor people were unreasonably crowded in the two wings, it was interesting to contemplate the difference between its present and former uses. Then it was the entrance into the darkness of hopeless bondage; now the vestibule of hoped-for freedom! . . .

They are quartered in small rooms, about 12 feet square, and average from 10 to 12 persons in each. They were generally associated together in families, and several families occasionally in one room. We were told that about two thirds are married.

All the able-bodied men and women, not obliged to take care of the children, are at work. The men earn about $20 per month, and the women from $2 to $6 per month, with rations. . . .

There was here an interesting school for boys and girls, taught by two colored teachers who had been educated in the North, and who were intelligent and efficient. The number of scholars was 160—half taught in the daytime and half in the evening. There were two rooms occupied by these schools—one about 12 by 15, and the other 10 by 12. The scholars paid 50 cents to $1 dollar per month each, and the school is self-sustaining. The pupils appeared to be well taught, and very promising. They read well, and apparently understood figures on the black board, although the school had been in operation only a few weeks.

Upon the whole, we regarded the condition of the refugees about Alexandria as very far from what it ought to be. In some respects it was not unfavorable; but in others it showed a want of attention to the ordinary requirements of tolerable existence. They expressed almost without exception, a preference for their present condition with freedom, to a more favorable one in slavery; because, as they said, they would have at least what they earned, and enjoy the fruits of their own labor; while in slavery, their masters took all and returned them but little. . . .

. . . We left Washington on the 28th, and reached Baltimore in time to take the evening boat, for Fort Monroe, where we arrived in the morning of the 29th. . . .

The number of refugees in this vicinity were reported to us as follows: We were informed that there were considerable numbers at Yorktown, Suffolk, and Portsmouth, but could not learn how many were there. The government gives employment to all the able-bodied men. Some of the women are employed also, but most of the women and children are without employment. The rate of wages, as we understood, was, at Fort Monroe, $10 per month, and rations. But little of the wages had been paid. The women and children have no rations here, and depend upon occasional employment and charity for subsistence. . . .

The men are said to work well. They are kept at work all day, and sometimes called upon to work at nights, and on the first day of the week, in cases of emergency. We were informed that they were treated very roughly; sometimes abused and maimed, by the brutality of those under whom they work. . . .

We attended the first part of a meeting for worship of the colored refugees, held at three o'clock, on the afternoon of the 30th. When we entered, they were all kneeling, at prayer; and one of them, in simple eloquence, was pleading at the throne of Infinite Mercy, for aid to overcome the evil of their hearts, and live in obedience to His law; that they might be enabled to bear with patience all the troubles of life, and when all was over, be received in mansions of eternal rest! They then united in singing. The air was plaintive, but the words were not understood by us. At its conclusion, they again knelt in prayer. After acknowledging the evil of their past lives, the speaker pleaded for mercy and forgiveness, and for help in the future. . . . Then he prayed for the President of the United States; that he might be preserved, comforted, and strengthened by Almighty power; that he might be endowed with wisdom, and enabled to perform the will of Heaven; also, for the Union and the rulers of the nation, and its armies;—that the Lord would be with them, and strengthen them to overcome all enemies, and re-establish the laws, and maintain the rights of all. . . .

We inquired of many where they came from, and why they left their masters. Generally the latter question seemed to excite surprise or incredulity, but the answer was nearly the same in all cases: they came away for their freedom, so that they might enjoy the reward of their own labor; but that if they could have this at home they would rather go back and live where they had lived. Not one of all the multitude, whom we saw, was desirous of going North. . . .

On our way from Washington, we learned from a gentleman well acquainted with North Carolina, that there is now a great scarcity of laborers in the northeastern part, in consequence of the escape of the slaves; and that many people there are suffering serious inconvenience and loss for want of their services.

We feel the vast importance of a correct and clear conclusion upon this branch of our inquiry, because it must have a controlling influence upon every honest man, whose opinion or action may affect the condition and welfare of millions of the human family. . . . The following are extracts from a letter published in the Alton Telegraph, and dated October 13th, 1862. Speaking of the refugees whom he had lately seen at Lawrence (Kansas), the writer says:

"As I learned that all the children of this school, had, within a few months, been rescued from Slavery, I expected to see a motley, lawless group of little, ragged, dirty children, something like those gathered up at the Five Points, in New York. But not a bit of it! Not a bit of it! For cleanliness, neatness, order, general good behavior, and apparent comfort, I have seldom seen a Sunday School that excelled it. Many of the little girls had neat straw bonnets, of the latest fashion, ornamented with a profusion of flowers and ribbons and with such regard to colors, too, as might repulse every suspicion of disloyalty. 'Why,' said I to the Superintendent, 'it must have cost the citizens a good deal of money to dress up all these children in this style.' 'Not a cent, not a cent, sir!' said he. 'Every one of these is dressed at the expense of their parents, from the proceeds of their own earnings since they have been here.'

"Most of them (the Negroes), in and about this town and vicinity, have emigrated from Missouri and Arkansas within a few months. Although they amount to many hundreds, not one, that I could learn of, has been a public expense. They readily get employment, and fair wages, which enables them at once to make themselves and families comfortable. A benevolent gentleman, on whom they are accustomed to call on their first entry into the place, usually tells them where they can get employment, and further inquires into their circumstances; and if he finds they need a shovel, an axe, or a pair of shoes he gives them an order on a store for such articles, and states, in the order, that if the bearer does not pay for them, in

a reasonable length of time, he will. This gentleman told me, that he had recently called at the store, to learn the state of his account, and he found of five or six hundred dollars charged to him on these orders within a few months, all but eight dollars had been paid by the contrabands themselves."

. . . We could adduce the testimony of many other witnesses to show the industry of these people, and the value of their labor, but it is deemed unnecessary. . . . When these people enjoy the rights and privileges of freemen, they are not only able to take care of themselves, but that they have, in some instances, by their industry, accomplished what few other men, under like circumstances, could equal, and perhaps none surpass. . . .

In reflecting upon the condition of the refugees, with a view of relieving their present wants and providing for their future support, it is evident that the chief reliance must be upon themselves. It is well that they have, in this respect, been cared for by their Maker, for vain would be the attempt of any government to provide for such a multitude! But so far as others are concerned, we have arrived at a simple conclusion. It is briefly comprehended in the command which is binding alike upon all Christians, whether Rulers, Statesmen, or People: "All things whatsoever ye would that men should do to you, do ye even so to them."

Document Fourteen

Lincoln's Position on Slavery Gradually Changes

Context: *The following documents chart Lincoln's evolving views on the relationship between slavery and the Civil War. Keep in mind that South Carolina and six other cotton states had already left the Union when he gave his first inaugural speech. Four years later, when he delivered his second inaugural speech, northerners could sense that the war was nearing the end.*

Questions to Consider: *What was Lincoln's primary concern during the first two years of the war? Why did Lincoln issue the Emancipation Proclamation and on what grounds did he defend emancipation? Had he become an unconditional abolitionist or was he trying to save the Union? Compare Lincoln's Second Inaugural Address with his first. How had his views about the war changed? Should we think of Lincoln as the Great Emancipator?*

Lincoln's First Inaugural Address (March 1861)

Fellow-Citizens of the United States:

In compliance with a custom as old as the Government itself, I appear before you to address you briefly and to take in your presence the oath prescribed by the Constitution of the United States to be taken by the President "before he enters on the execution of this office." I do not consider it necessary at present for me to discuss those matters of administration about which there is no special anxiety or excitement.

Apprehension seems to exist among the people of the Southern States that by the accession of a Republican Administration their property and their peace and personal security are to be endangered. There has never been any reasonable cause for such apprehension. Indeed, the most ample evidence to the contrary has all the while existed and been open to their inspection. It is found in nearly all the published speeches of him who now addresses you. I do but quote from one of those speeches when I declare that:

I have no purpose, directly or indirectly, to interfere with the institution of slavery in the States where it exists. I believe I have no lawful right to do so, and I have no inclination to do so.

Lincoln's Position on Slavery Gradually Changes   69

Those who nominated and elected me did so with full knowledge that I had made this and many similar declarations and had never recanted them; and more than this, they placed in the platform for my acceptance, and as a law to themselves and to me, the clear and emphatic resolution which I now read:

Resolved, That the maintenance inviolate of the rights of the States, and especially the right of each State to order and control its own domestic institutions according to its own judgment exclusively, is essential to that balance of power on which the perfection and endurance of our political fabric depend; and we denounce the lawless invasion by armed force of the soil of any State or Territory, no matter what pretext, as among the gravest of crimes.

I now reiterate these sentiments, and in doing so I only press upon the public attention the most conclusive evidence of which the case is susceptible that the property, peace, and security of no section are to be in any wise endangered by the now incoming Administration. I add, too, that all the protection which, consistently with the Constitution and the laws, can be given will be cheerfully given to all the States when lawfully demanded, for whatever cause— as cheerfully to one section as to another.

There is much controversy about the delivering up of fugitives from service or labor. The clause I now read is as plainly written in the Constitution as any other of its provisions:

> *No person held to service or labor in one State, under the laws*
> *thereof, escaping into another, shall in consequence of any law or*
> *regulation therein be discharged from such service or labor, but*
> *shall be delivered up on claim of the party to whom such service*
> *or labor may be due.*

It is scarcely questioned that this provision was intended by those who made it for the reclaiming of what we call fugitive slaves; and the intention of the lawgiver is the law. . . .

There is some difference of opinion whether this clause should be enforced by national or by State authority, but surely that difference is not a very material one. If the slave is to be surrendered, it can be of but little consequence to him or to others by which authority it is done. . . .

Again: In any law upon this subject ought not all the safeguards of liberty known in civilized and humane jurisprudence to be introduced, so that a free man be not in any case surrendered as a slave? And might it not be well at the same time to provide by law for the enforcement of that clause in the Constitution which guarantees that "the citizens of each State shall be entitled to all privileges and immunities of citizens in the several States"? . . .

It is seventy-two years since the first inauguration of a President under our National Constitution. During that period fifteen different and greatly distinguished citizens have in succession administered the executive branch of the Government. They have conducted it through many perils, and generally with great success. Yet, with all this scope of precedent, I now enter upon the same task for the brief constitutional term of four years under great and peculiar difficulty. A disruption of the Federal Union, heretofore only menaced, is now formidably attempted.

I hold that in contemplation of universal law and of the Constitution the Union of these States is perpetual. Perpetuity is implied, if not expressed, in the fundamental law of all national governments. It is safe to assert that no government proper ever had a provision in its organic law for its own termination. Continue to execute all the express provisions of our National Constitution, and the Union will endure forever, it being impossible to destroy it except by some action not provided for in the instrument itself.

Again: If the United States be not a government proper, but an association of States in the nature of contract merely, can it, as a contract, be peaceably unmade by less than all the parties who made it? One party to a contract may violate it—break it, so to speak—but does it not require all to lawfully rescind it? . . .

. . . no State upon its own mere motion can lawfully get out of the Union; that resolves and ordinances to that effect are legally void, and that acts of violence within any State or States against the authority of the United States are insurrectionary or revolutionary, according to circumstances.

I therefore consider that in view of the Constitution and the laws the Union is unbroken, and to the extent of my ability, I shall take care, as the Constitution itself expressly enjoins upon me, that the laws of the Union be faithfully executed in all the States. Doing this I deem to be only a simple duty on my part, and I shall perform it so far as practicable unless my rightful masters, the American people, shall withhold the requisite means or in some authoritative manner direct the contrary. I trust this will not be regarded as a menace, but only as the declared purpose of the Union that it will constitutionally defend and maintain itself.

In doing this there needs to be no bloodshed or violence, and there shall be none unless it be forced upon the national authority. The power confided to me will be used to hold, occupy, and possess the property and places belonging to the Government and to collect the duties and imposts; but beyond what may be necessary for these objects, there will be no invasion, no using of force against or among the people anywhere. Where hostility to the United States in any interior locality shall be so great and universal as to prevent competent resident citizens from holding the Federal offices, there will be no attempt to force obnoxious strangers among the people for that object. While the strict legal right may exist in the Government to enforce the exercise of these offices, the attempt to do so would be so irritating and so nearly impracticable withal that I deem it better to forego for the time the uses of such offices.

The mails, unless repelled, will continue to be furnished in all parts of the Union. So far as possible the people everywhere shall have that sense of perfect security which is most favorable to calm thought and reflection. . . .

That there are persons in one section or another who seek to destroy the Union at all events and are glad of any pretext to do it I will neither affirm nor deny; but if there be such, I need address no word to them. To those, however, who really love the Union may I not speak?

Before entering upon so grave a matter as the destruction of our national fabric, with all its benefits, its memories, and its hopes, would it not be wise to ascertain precisely why we do it? Will you hazard so desperate a step while there is any possibility that any portion of the ills you fly from have no real existence? Will you, while the certain ills you fly to are greater than all the real ones you fly from, will you risk the commission of so fearful a mistake?

All profess to be content in the Union if all constitutional rights can be maintained. Is it true, then, that any right plainly written in the Constitution has been denied? I think not. . . . If by the mere force of numbers a majority should deprive a minority of any clearly written constitutional right, it might in a moral point of view justify revolution; certainly would if such right were a vital one. But such is not our case. All the vital rights of minorities and of individuals are so plainly assured to them by affirmations and negations, guaranties and prohibitions, in the Constitution that controversies never arise concerning them. . . . No foresight can anticipate nor any document of reasonable length contain express provisions for all possible questions. Shall fugitives from labor be surrendered by national or by State authority? The Constitution does not expressly say. May Congress prohibit slavery in the Territories? The Constitution does not expressly say. Must Congress protect slavery in the Territories? The Constitution does not expressly say.

From questions of this class spring all our constitutional controversies, and we divide upon them into majorities and minorities. If the minority will not acquiesce, the majority must, or the Government must cease. There is no other alternative, for continuing the Government is acquiescence on one side or the other. If a minority in such case will secede rather than acquiesce, they make a precedent which in turn will divide and ruin them, for a minority of their own will secede from them whenever a majority refuses to be controlled by such minority. . . .

Is there such perfect identity of interests among the States to compose a new union as to produce harmony only and prevent renewed secession?

Plainly the central idea of secession is the essence of anarchy. A majority held in restraint by constitutional checks and limitations, and always changing easily with deliberate changes of popular opinions and sentiments, is the only true sovereign of a free people. Whoever rejects it does of necessity fly to anarchy or to despotism. Unanimity is impossible. The rule of a minority, as a permanent arrangement, is wholly inadmissible; so that, rejecting the majority principle, anarchy or despotism in some form is all that is left. . . .

One section of our country believes slavery is right and ought to be extended, while the other believes it is wrong and ought not to be extended. This is the only substantial dispute. The fugitive-slave clause of the Constitution and the law for the suppression of the foreign slave trade are each as well enforced, perhaps, as any law can ever be in a community where the moral sense of the people imperfectly supports the law itself. The great body of the people abide by the dry legal obligation in both cases, and a few break over in each. This, I think, can not be perfectly cured, and it would be worse in both cases after the separation of the sections than before. The foreign slave trade, now imperfectly suppressed, would be ultimately revived without restriction in one section, while fugitive slaves, now only partially surrendered, would not be surrendered at all by the other.

Physically speaking, we can not separate. We can not remove our respective sections from each other nor build an impassable wall between them. A husband and wife may be divorced and go out of the presence and beyond the reach of each other, but the different parts of our country can not do this. They can not but remain face to face, and intercourse, either amicable or hostile, must continue between them. . . . Suppose you go to war, you can not fight always; and when, after much loss on both sides and no gain on either, you cease fighting, the identical old questions, as to terms of intercourse, are again upon you.

This country, with its institutions, belongs to the people who inhabit it. Whenever they shall grow weary of the existing Government, they can exercise their constitutional right of amending it or their revolutionary right to dismember or overthrow it. I can not be ignorant of the fact that many worthy and patriotic citizens are desirous of having the National Constitution amended. While I make no recommendation of amendments, I fully recognize the rightful authority of the people over the whole subject, to be exercised in either of the modes prescribed in the instrument itself; and I should, under existing circumstances, favor rather than oppose a fair opportunity being afforded the people to act upon it. I will venture to add that to me the convention mode seems preferable, in that it allows amendments to originate with the people themselves, instead of only permitting them to take or reject propositions originated by others. . . I understand a proposed amendment to the Constitution—which amendment, however, I have not seen—has passed Congress, to the effect that the Federal Government shall never interfere with the domestic institutions of the States, including that of persons held to service. To avoid misconstruction of what I have said, I depart from my purpose not to speak of particular amendments so far as to say that, holding such a provision to now be implied constitutional law, I have no objection to its being made express and irrevocable. . . .

Why should there not be a patient confidence in the ultimate justice of the people? Is there any better or equal hope in the world? In our present differences, is either party without faith of being in the right? If the Almighty Ruler of Nations, with His eternal truth and justice, be on your side of the North, or on yours of the South, that truth and that justice will surely prevail by the judgment of this great tribunal of the American people.

By the frame of the Government under which we live this same people have wisely given their public servants but little power for mischief, and have with equal wisdom provided for the return of that little to their own hands at very short intervals. While the people retain their virtue and vigilance no Administration by any extreme of wickedness or folly can very seriously injure the Government in the short space of four years.

My countrymen, one and all, think calmly and well upon this whole subject. Nothing valuable can be lost by taking time. If there be an object to hurry any of you in hot haste to a step which you would never take deliberately, that object will be frustrated by taking time; but no good object can be frustrated by it. . . .

In your hands, my dissatisfied fellow-countrymen, and not in mine, is the momentous issue of civil war. The Government will not assail you. You can have no conflict without being yourselves the aggressors. You have no oath registered in heaven to destroy the Government, while I shall have the most solemn one to "preserve, protect, and defend it."

I am loath to close. We are not enemies, but friends. We must not be enemies. Though passion may have strained it must not break our bonds of affection. The mystic chords of memory, stretching from every battlefield and patriot grave to every living heart and hearthstone all over this broad land, will yet swell the chorus of the Union, when again touched, as surely they will be, by the better angels of our nature.

Letter to Horace Greeley, August 1862

Executive Mansion,
Washington, August 22, 1862.
Hon. Horace Greeley:

Dear Sir:

I have just read yours of the 19th. addressed to myself through the *New-York Tribune*. If there be in it any statements, or assumptions of fact, which I may know to be erroneous, I do not, now and here, controvert them. If there be in it any inferences which I may believe to be falsely drawn, I do not now and here, argue against them. If there be perceptable [sic] in it an impatient and dictatorial tone, I waive it in deference to an old friend, whose heart I have always supposed to be right.

As to the policy I "seem to be pursuing" as you say, I have not meant to leave any one in doubt. [*Editor's note: Greeley has anticipated that Lincoln is ready to emancipate the slaves.*]

I would save the Union. I would save it the shortest way under the Constitution. The sooner the national authority can be restored; the nearer the Union will be "the Union as it was." If there be those who would not save the Union, unless they could at the same time save slavery,

I do not agree with them. If there be those who would not save the Union unless they could at the same time destroy slavery, I do not agree with them. My paramount object in this struggle is to save the Union, and is not either to save or to destroy slavery. If I could save the Union without freeing any slave I would do it, and if I could save it by freeing all the slaves I would do it; and if I could save it by freeing some and leaving others alone I would also do that. What I do about slavery, and the colored race, I do because I believe it helps to save the Union; and what I forbear, I forbear because I do not believe it would help to save the Union. I shall do less whenever I shall believe what I am doing hurts the cause, and I shall do more whenever I shall believe doing more will help the cause. I shall try to correct errors when shown to be errors; and I shall adopt new views so fast as they shall appear to be true views.

I have here stated my purpose according to my view of official duty; and I intend no modification of my oft-expressed personal wish that all men everywhere could be free.

Yours,
A. Lincoln.

Emancipation Proclamation, January 1863

By the President of the United States of America:

A Proclamation.

Whereas, on the twenty second day of September, in the year of our Lord one thousand eight hundred and sixty two, a proclamation was issued by the President of the United States, containing, among other things, the following, to wit:

"That on the first day of January, in the year of our Lord one thousand eight hundred and sixty-three, all persons held as slaves within any State or designated part of a State, the people whereof shall then be in rebellion against the United States, shall be then, thenceforward, and forever free; and the Executive Government of the United States, including the military and naval authority thereof, will recognize and maintain the freedom of such persons, and will do no act or acts to repress such persons, or any of them, in any efforts they may make for their actual freedom.

"That the Executive will, on the first day of January aforesaid, by proclamation, designate the States and parts of States, if any, in which the people thereof, respectively, shall then be in rebellion against the United States; and the fact that any State, or the people thereof, shall on that day be, in good faith, represented in the Congress of the United States by members chosen thereto at elections wherein a majority of the qualified voters of such State shall have participated, shall, in the absence of strong countervailing testimony, be deemed conclusive evidence that such State, and the people thereof, are not then in rebellion against the United States."

Now, therefore I, Abraham Lincoln, President of the United States, by virtue of the power in me vested as Commander-in-Chief, of the Army and Navy of the United States in time of actual armed rebellion against the authority and government of the United States, and as a fit and necessary war measure for suppressing said rebellion, do, on this first day of January, in the year of our Lord one thousand eight hundred and sixty three, and in accordance with my purpose so to do publicly proclaimed for the full period of one hundred days, from the day first above mentioned, order and designate as the States and parts of States wherein the people thereof respectively, are this day in rebellion against the United States, the following, to wit:

Arkansas, Texas, Louisiana, (except the Parishes of St. Bernard, Plaquemines, Jefferson, St. Johns, St. Charles, St. James Ascension, Assumption, Terrebonne, Lafourche, St. Mary, St. Martin, and Orleans, including the City of New Orleans) Mississippi, Alabama, Florida, Georgia, South-Carolina, North-Carolina, and Virginia, (except the forty eight counties designated as West Virginia, and also the counties of Berkley, Accomac, Northampton, Elizabeth-City, York, Princess Ann, and Norfolk, including the cities of Norfolk and Portsmouth), and which excepted parts, are for the present, left precisely as if this proclamation were not issued.

And by virtue of the power, and for the purpose aforesaid, I do order and declare that all persons held as slaves within said designated States, and parts of States, are, and henceforward shall be free; and that the Executive government of the United States, including the military and naval authorities thereof, will recognize and maintain the freedom of said persons.

And I hereby enjoin upon the people so declared to be free to abstain from all violence, unless in necessary self-defense; and I recommend to them that, in all cases when allowed, they labor faithfully for reasonable wages.

And I further declare and make known, that such persons of suitable condition, will be received into the armed service of the United States to garrison forts, positions, stations, and other places, and to man vessels of all sorts in said service.

And upon this act, sincerely believed to be an act of justice, warranted by the Constitution, upon military necessity, I invoke the considerate judgment of mankind, and the gracious favor of Almighty God.

In witness whereof, I have hereunto set my hand and caused the seal of the United States to be affixed. Done at the City of Washington, this first day of January, in the year of our Lord one thousand eight hundred and sixty three, and of the Independence of the United States of America the eighty-seventh.

Letter to James C. Conkling (August 1863)

Executive Mansion,
Washington, August 26, 1863.
Hon. James C. Conkling

My Dear Sir. [*Editor's note: This letter was written to be read as a speech in Lincoln's absence.*]

Your letter inviting me to attend a mass-meeting of unconditional Union-men, to be held at the Capitol of Illinois, on the 3rd day of September, has been received.

It would be very agreeable to me, to thus meet my old friends, at my own home; but I can not, just now, be absent from here, so long as a visit there, would require.

The meeting is to be of all those who maintain unconditional devotion to the Union; and I am sure my old political friends will thank me for tendering, as I do, the nation's gratitude to those other noble men, whom no partizan malice, or partizan hope, can make false to the nation's life.

There are those who are dissatisfied with me. To such I would say: You desire peace; and you blame me that we do not have it. But how can we attain it? There are but three conceivable ways. First, to suppress the rebellion by force of arms. This I am trying to do. Are you for it? If you are, so far we are agreed. If you are not for it, a second way is to give up the Union. I am against this. Are you for it? If you are, you should say so plainly. If you are not for force, nor yet for dissolution, there only remains some imaginable compromise. I do not believe any compromise, embracing the maintenance of the Union, is now possible. All I learn, leads to a directly opposite belief. The strength of the rebellion, is its military—its army. That army dominates all the country, and all the people, within its range. Any offer of terms made by any man or men within that range, in opposition to that army, is simply nothing for the present; because such man or men, have no power whatever to enforce their side of a compromise, if one were made with them. . . .

But to be plain, you are dissatisfied with me about the negro. Quite likely there is a difference of opinion between you and myself upon that subject. I certainly wish that all men could be free, while I suppose you do not. Yet I have neither adopted, nor proposed any measure, which is not consistent with even your view, provided you are for the Union. I suggested compensated emancipation; to which you replied you wished not to be taxed to buy negroes. But I had not asked you to be taxed to buy negroes, except in such way, as to save you from greater taxation to save the Union exclusively by other means.

You dislike the emancipation proclamation; and, perhaps, would have it retracted. You say it is unconstitutional—I think differently. I think the constitution invests its Commander-in-chief, with the law of war, in time of war. The most that can be said, if so much, is, that slaves are property. Is there—has there ever been—any question that by the law of war, property, both of enemies and friends, may be taken when needed? And is it not needed whenever taking it, helps us, or hurts the enemy? Armies, the world over, destroy enemies' property when they can not use it; and even destroy their own to keep it from the enemy. Civilized belligerents do all in their power to help themselves, or hurt the enemy, except a few things regarded as barbarous or cruel. Among the exceptions are the massacre of vanquished foes, and non-combatants, male and female.

But the proclamation, as law, either is valid, or is not valid. If it is not valid, it needs no retraction. If it is valid, it can not be retracted, any more than the dead can be brought to life. Some of you profess to think its retraction would operate favorably for the Union. Why better after the retraction, than before the issue? There was more than a year and a half of trial to suppress the rebellion before the proclamation issued, the last one hundred days of which passed under an explicit notice that it was coming, unless averted by those in revolt, returning to their allegiance. The war has certainly progressed as favorably for us, since the issue of proclamation as before. I know, as fully as one can know the opinions of others, that some of the commanders of our armies in the field who have given us our most important successes believe the emancipation policy and the use of the colored troops constitute the heaviest blow yet dealt to the Rebellion, and that at least one of these important successes could not have been achieved when it was but for the aid of black soldiers. Among the commanders holding these views are some who have never had any affinity with what is called abolitionism or with the Republican party policies but who held them purely as military opinions. I submit these opinions as being entitled to some weight against the objections often urged that emancipation and arming the blacks are unwise as military measures and were not adopted as such in good faith.

You say you will not fight to free negroes. Some of them seem willing to fight for you; but, no matter. Fight you, then exclusively to save the Union. I issued the proclamation on purpose to aid you in saving the Union. Whenever you shall have conquered all resistence to the Union, if I shall urge you to continue fighting, it will be an apt time, then, for you to declare you will not fight to free negroes.

I thought that in your struggle for the Union, to whatever extent the negroes should cease helping the enemy, to that extent it weakened the enemy in his resistance to you. Do you think differently? I thought that whatever negroes can be got to do as soldiers, leaves just so much less for white soldiers to do, in saving the Union. Does it appear otherwise to you? But negroes, like other people, act upon motives. Why should they do any thing for us, if we will do nothing for them? If they stake their lives for us, they must be prompted by the strongest motive—even the promise of freedom. And the promise being made, must be kept.

The signs look better. The Father of Waters again goes unvexed to the sea. Thanks to the great Northwest for it. Nor yet wholly to them. Three hundred miles up, they met New England, Empire, Keystone, and Jersey, hewing their way right and left. The Sunny South too, in more colors than one, also lent a hand. On the spot, their part of the history was jotted down in black and white. The job was a great national one; and let none be banned who bore an honorable part in it. And while those who have cleared the great river may well be proud, even that is not all. It is hard to say that anything has been more bravely, and well done, than at Antietam, Murfreesboro, Gettysburg, and on many fields of lesser note. Nor must Uncle Sam's web-feet be forgotten. At all the watery margins they have been present. Not only on the deep sea, the broad bay, and the rapid river, but also up the narrow muddy bayou, and wherever the ground was a little damp, they have been, and made their tracks. Thanks to all. For the great republic—for the principle it lives by, and keeps alive—for man's vast future—thanks to all.

Peace does not appear so distant as it did. I hope it will come soon, and come to stay; and so come as to be worth the keeping in all future time. It will then have been proved that, among free men, there can be no successful appeal from the ballot to the bullet; and that they who take such appeal are sure to lose their case, and pay the cost. And then, there will be some black men who can remember that, with silent tongue, and clenched teeth, and steady eye, and well-poised bayonet, they have helped mankind on to this great consummation; while, I fear, there will be some white ones, unable to forget that, with malignant heart, and deceitful speech, they strove to hinder it.

Still, let us not be over-sanguine of a speedy final triumph. Let us be quite sober. Let us diligently apply the means, never doubting that a just God, in his own good time, will give us the rightful result.

Lincoln's Second Inaugural, March 1865

Fellow-Countrymen:

At this second appearing to take the oath of the Presidential office there is less occasion for an extended address than there was at the first. Then a statement somewhat in detail of a course to be pursued seemed fitting and proper. Now, at the expiration of four years, during which public declarations have been constantly called forth on every point and phase of the great contest which still absorbs the attention and engrosses the energies of the nation, little that is new could be presented. The progress of our arms, upon which all else chiefly depends, is as well known to the public as to myself, and it is, I trust, reasonably satisfactory and encouraging to all. With high hope for the future, no prediction in regard to it is ventured.

On the occasion corresponding to this four years ago all thoughts were anxiously directed to an impending civil war. All dreaded it, all sought to avert it. While the inaugural address was being delivered from this place, devoted altogether to saving the Union without war, urgent agents were in the city seeking to destroy it without war—seeking to dissolve the Union and divide effects by negotiation. Both parties deprecated war, but one of them would make war rather than let the nation survive, and the other would accept war rather than let it perish, and the war came.

One-eighth of the whole population were colored slaves, not distributed generally over the Union, but localized in the southern part of it. These slaves constituted a peculiar and powerful interest. All knew that this interest was somehow the cause of the war. To strengthen, perpetuate, and extend this interest was the object for which the insurgents would rend the Union even by war, while the Government claimed no right to do more than to restrict the territorial enlargement of it. Neither party expected for the war the magnitude or the duration which it has already attained. Neither anticipated that the cause of the conflict might cease with or even before the conflict itself should cease. Each looked for an easier triumph, and a result less fundamental and astounding. Both read the same Bible and pray to the same God, and each invokes His aid against the other. It may seem strange that any men should dare to ask a just God's assistance in wringing their bread from the sweat of other men's faces, but let us judge not, that we be not judged. The prayers of both could not be answered. That of neither has been answered fully. The Almighty has His own purposes. "Woe unto the world because of offenses; for it must needs be that offenses come, but woe to that man by whom the offense cometh." If we shall suppose that American slavery is one of those offenses which, in the providence of God, must needs come, but which, having continued through His appointed time, He now wills to remove, and that He gives to both North and South this terrible war as the woe due to those by whom the offense came, shall we discern therein any departure from those divine attributes which the believers in a living God always ascribe to Him? Fondly do we hope, fervently do we pray, that this mighty scourge of war may speedily pass away. Yet, if God wills that it continue until all the wealth piled by the bondsman's two hundred and fifty years of unrequited toil shall be sunk, and until every drop of blood drawn with the lash shall be paid by another drawn with the sword, as was said three thousand years ago, so still it must be said "the judgments of the Lord are true and righteous altogether."

With malice toward none, with charity for all, with firmness in the right as God gives us to see the right, let us strive on to finish the work we are in, to bind up the nation's wounds, to care for him who shall have borne the battle and for his widow and his orphan, to do all which may achieve and cherish a just and lasting peace among ourselves and with all nations.

Document Fifteen

Frederick Douglass Advocates Suffrage for African Americans

Context: *As one of America's foremost abolitionists, Frederick Douglass hoped to turn the Civil War into a civil rights crusade. This speech was given in Boston before a largely sympathetic crowd. Keep in mind that Douglass was also a delegate at the Seneca Falls convention, where he had forcefully advocated women's suffrage.*

Questions to Consider: *According to Douglass, how did the slaves respond to the Civil War? Why did that response justify voting rights for blacks? What pragmatic arguments for black suffrage did Douglass make for his primarily white audience?*

Frederick Douglass, "What the Black Man Wants," (1864)

. . . I have had but one idea for the last three years, to present to the American people, and the phraseology in which I clothe it is the old abolition phraseology. I am for the "immediate, unconditional, and universal" enfranchisement of the black man, in every State in the Union. (Loud applause.) Without this, his liberty is a mockery; without this, you might as well almost retain the old name of slavery for his condition; for, in fact, if he is not the slave of the individual master, he is the slave of society, and holds his liberty as a privilege, not as a right. He is at the mercy of the mob, and has no means of protecting himself.

It may be objected, however, that this pressing of the negro's right to suffrage is premature. Let us have slavery abolished, it may be said, let us have labor organized, and then, in the natural course of events, the right of suffrage will be extended to the negro. I do not agree with this. The constitution of the human mind is such, that if it once disregards the conviction forced upon it by a revelation of truth, it requires the exercise of a higher power to produce the same conviction afterwards. The American people are now in tears. The Shenandoah has run blood—the best blood of the North. All around Richmond, the blood of New England and of the North has been shed—of your sons, your brothers and your fathers. We all feel, in the existence of this Rebellion, that judgments terrible, wide-spread, far-reaching, overwhelming, are abroad in the land; and we feel, in view of these judgments, just now, a disposition to learn righteousness. This is the hour. Our streets are in mourning, tears are falling at every fireside, and under the chastisement of this Rebellion we have almost come up to the point of conceding this great, this all-important right of suffrage. I fear that if we fail to do it now, if abolitionists fail to press it now, we may not see, for centuries to come, the same disposition that exists at this moment. (Applause.) Hence, I say, now is the time to press this right.

It may be asked, "Why do you want it? Some men have got along very well without it. Women have not this right." Shall we justify one wrong by another? That is a sufficient answer. Shall we at this moment justify the deprivation of the negro of the right to vote, because some one else is deprived of that privilege? I hold that women, as well as men, have the right to vote (applause), and my heart and my voice go with the movement to extend suffrage to woman; but that question rests upon another basis than that on which our right rests. We may be asked, I say, why we want it. I will tell you why we want it. We want it because it is our right, first of all. (Applause.) No class of men can, without insulting their own nature, be content with any deprivation of their rights. We want it, again, as a means for educating our race. Men are so constituted that they derive their conviction of their own possibilities largely from the estimate formed of them by others. If nothing is expected of a people, that people will find it difficult to contradict that expectation. By depriving us of suffrage, you affirm our incapacity to form an intelligent judgment respecting public men and public measures; you declare before the world that we are unfit to exercise the elective franchise, and by this means lead us to under-value ourselves, to put a low estimate upon ourselves, and to feel that we have no possibilities like other men. Again, I want the elective franchise, for one, as a colored man, because ours is a peculiar government, based upon a peculiar idea, and that idea is universal suffrage. . . . [W]here universal suffrage is the rule, where that is the fundamental idea of the Government, to rule us out is to make us an exception, to brand us with the stigma of inferiority, and to invite to our heads the missiles of those about us; therefore, I want the franchise for the black man.

There are, however, other reasons, not derived from any consideration merely of our rights, but arising out of the condition of the South, and of the country—considerations which have already been referred to by Mr. Phillips—considerations which must arrest the attention of statesmen. I believe that when the tall heads of this Rebellion shall have been swept down, as they will be swept down, when the Davises and Toombses and Stephenses, and others who are leading in this Rebellion shall have been blotted out, there will be this rank undergrowth of treason, to which reference has been made, growing up there, and interfering with, and thwarting the quiet operation of the Federal Government in those States. You will see those traitors handing down, from sire to son, the same malignant spirit which they have manifested, and which they are now exhibiting, with malicious hearts, broad blades, and bloody hands in the field, against our sons and brothers. That spirit will still remain; and whoever sees the Federal Government extended over those Southern States will see that Government in a strange land, and not only in a strange land, but in an enemy's land. . . . That enmity will not die out in a year, will not die out in an age. . . . They will endeavor to circumvent, they will endeavor to destroy, the peaceful operation of this Government. Now, where will you find the strength to counterbalance this spirit, if you do not find it in the negroes of the South? They are your friends, and have always been your friends. They were your friends even when the Government did not regard them as such. They comprehended the genius of this war before you did. It is a significant fact, it is a marvelous fact, it seems almost to imply a direct inter-position of Providence, that this war, which began in the interest of slavery on both sides, bids fair to end in the interest of liberty on both sides. (Applause.) It was begun, I say, in the interest of slavery on both sides. The South was fighting to take slavery out of the Union, and the North fighting to keep it in the Union; the South fighting to get it beyond the limits of the United-States Constitution, and the North fighting to retain it within those limits; the South fighting for new guarantees, and the North fighting for the old guarantees;—both despising the negro, both insulting the negro. Yet, the negro, apparently endowed with wisdom from on high, saw more clearly the end from the beginning than we did. When Seward said the status of no man in the country would be changed by the war, the negro did not believe him. (Applause.) When our generals sent their underlings in shoulder-straps to hunt the flying negro back from our lines into the jaws of slavery, from which he had escaped, the negroes thought that a mistake had been made, and that the intentions of the Government had not been rightly understood by our officers in shoulder-straps, and they continued to come into our lines, threading their way through bogs and fens, over briers and thorns, fording streams, swimming rivers, bringing us tidings as to the safe path to march, and pointing out the dangers that threatened us. They are our only friends in the South, and we should be true to them in this their trial hour, and see to it that they have the elective franchise.

I know that we are inferior to you in some things—virtually inferior. We walk about among you like dwarfs among giants. Our heads are scarcely seen above the great sea of humanity. The Germans are superior to us; the Irish are superior to us; the Yankees are superior to us (laughter); they can do what we cannot, that is, what we have not hitherto been allowed to do. But while I make this admission, I utterly deny that we are originally, or naturally, or practically, or in any way, or in any important sense, inferior to anybody on this globe (Loud applause). This charge of inferiority is an old dodge. It has been made available for oppression on many occasions. It is only about six centuries since the blue-eyed and fair-haired Anglo-Saxons were considered inferior by the haughty Normans, who once trampled upon them. If you read the history of the Norman Conquest, you will find that this proud Anglo-Saxon was once looked upon as of coarser clay than his Norman master, and might be found in the highways and byways of old England laboring with a brass collar on his neck, and the name of his master marked upon it. You were down then! (Laughter and applause) You are up now. I am glad you are up, and I want you to be glad to help us up also (Applause).

The story of our inferiority is an old dodge, as I have said; for wherever men oppress their fellows, wherever they enslave them, they will endeavor to find the needed apology for such enslavement and oppression in the character of the people oppressed and enslaved. When we wanted, a few years ago, a slice of Mexico, it was hinted that the Mexicans were an inferior race, that the old Castilian blood had become so weak that it would scarcely run down hill, and that Mexico needed the long, strong and beneficent arm of the Anglo-Saxon care extended over it. We said that it was necessary to its salvation, and a part of the "manifest destiny" of this Republic, to extend our arm over that dilapidated government. So, too, when Russia wanted to take possession of a part of the Ottoman Empire, the Turks were "an inferior race." So, too, when England wants to set the heel of her power more firmly in the quivering heart of old Ireland, the Celts are an "inferior race." So, too, the negro, when he is to be robbed of any right which is justly his, is an "inferior man." It is said that we are ignorant; I admit it. But if we know enough to be hung, we know enough to vote. If the negro knows enough to pay taxes to support the government, he knows enough to vote; taxation and representation should go together. If he knows enough to shoulder a musket and fight for the flag, fight for the government, he knows enough to vote. If he knows as much when he is sober as an Irishman knows when drunk, he knows enough to vote, on good American principles (Laughter and applause)....

I hold that the American government has taken upon itself a solemn obligation of honor, to see that this war—let it be long or let it be short, let it cost much or let it cost little—that this war shall not cease until every freedman at the South has the right to vote (Applause). It has bound itself to it. What have you asked the black men of the South, the black men of the whole country, to do? Why, you have asked them to incur the deadly enmity of their masters, in order to befriend you and to befriend this Government. You have asked us to call down, not only upon ourselves, but upon our children's children, the deadly hate of the entire Southern people. You have called upon us to turn our backs upon our masters, to abandon their cause and espouse yours; to turn against the South and in favor of the North; to shoot down the Confederacy and uphold the flag—the American flag. You have called upon us to expose ourselves to all the subtle machinations of their malignity for all time. And now, what do you propose to do when you come to make peace? To reward your enemies, and trample in the dust your friends? Do you intend to sacrifice the very men who have come to the rescue of your banner in the South, and incurred the lasting displeasure of their masters thereby? Do you intend to sacrifice them and reward your enemies? Do you mean to give your enemies the right to vote, and take it away from your friends? Is that wise policy? Is that honorable? Could American honor withstand such a blow? I do not believe you will do it. I think you will see to it that we have the right to vote. There is something too mean in looking upon the negro, when you are in trouble, as a citizen, and when you are free from trouble, as an alien. When this nation was in trouble, in its early struggles, it looked upon the negro as a citizen. In 1776 he was a citizen. At the time of the formation of the Constitution the negro had the right to vote in eleven States out of the old thirteen. In your trouble you have made us citizens. In 1812 Gen. Jackson addressed us as citizens—"fellow-citizens." He wanted us to fight. We were citizens then! And now, when you come to frame a conscription bill, the negro is a citizen again. He has been a citizen just three times in the history of this government, and it has always been in time of trouble. In time of trouble we are citizens. Shall we be citizens in war, and aliens in peace? Would that be just?

. . . Let me not be misunderstood here. I am not asking for sympathy at the hands of abolitionists, sympathy at the hands of any. I think the American people are disposed often to be generous rather than just. I look over this country at the present time, and I see Educational Societies, Sanitary Commissions, Freedmen's Associations, and the like, all very good: but in regard to the colored people there is always more that is benevolent, I perceive, than just, manifested towards us. What I ask for the negro is not benevolence, not pity, not sympathy, but simply justice. . . . Let him live or die by that. If you will only untie his hands, and give him a chance, I think he will live. He will work as readily for himself as the white man. A great many delusions have been swept away by this war. One was, that the negro would not work; he has proved his ability to work. Another was, that the negro would not fight; that he possessed only the most sheepish attributes of humanity; was a perfect lamb, or an "Uncle Tom;" disposed to take off his coat whenever required, fold his hands, and be whipped by anybody who wanted to whip him. But the war has proved that there is a great deal of human nature in the negro, and that "he will fight," as Mr. Quincy, our President, said, in earlier days than these, "when there is a reasonable probability of his whipping anybody. (Laughter and applause).

Document Sixteen

"Emancipation" by Thomas Nast

Context: *Thomas Nast, an influential political cartoonist whose work regularly appeared in the magazine* Harper's Weekly *from 1862 to 1886, used his talents as an illustrator to battle political corruption and build support for the Union during the Civil War. President Abraham Lincoln was so impressed with Nast's efforts on the Union's behalf that he heralded Nast as "our best recruiting sergeant." During the 1860s and 1870s, Nast's political cartoons supported the abolition of slavery, opposed racial segregation, and condemned the violence of the Ku Klux Klan. Nast's illustration "Emancipation" first appeared in* Harper's Weekly *on January 24, 1863, a few weeks after Lincoln issued the Emancipation Proclamation. In 1865, a Philadelphia printing company reissued the popular illustration as a print. The 1865 reprint replaced an illustration of the angels breaking a slave's chains that appeared at the bottom of the 1863 original with a portrait of Lincoln. The reprint stands as an example of how Americans began to reimagine Lincoln as the revered Great Emancipator in the wake of his assassination. In the 1863 version, Lincoln still occupied a meaningful, though less conspicuous, place of honor, The painting you see hanging on the wall in the central domestic scene is a portrait of Lincoln.*

Questions to Consider: *How does Nast envision the future of the freedmen and freewomen and how does he contrast that future with their enslaved past? In what ways does he employ domestic ideology, free labor ideology, and religious symbolism to illustrate the promise and justness of emancipation? What similarities and differences do you see between Frederick Douglass's antislavery appeal and Nast's visual representation of slavery's evils and emancipation's promise? How might Frederick Douglass have drawn the illustration differently? Based on your interpretation of the illustration, what kinds of Reconstruction policies do you think might have won Nast's sympathy?*

THOMAS NAST, "EMANCIPATION" (1865)

© *Everett Historical/Shutterstock.com*

Name: _____ Date: _____

Document Analysis Worksheet

1. Date/Author of Document/Author's Position: Intended Audience:

2. Why was this document written? List three points the author made that you find important.

3. List two things the document tells you about life in the United States at the time it was written.

4. Write a question to the author that the document left unanswered.

Name: _____ Date: _____

Comparative Analysis Worksheet

Choose two documents from this week's readings in which the document authors present different takes on a particular issue.

    1. Identify two or three key points on which the authors agree and/or disagree.

_____

_____

_____

_____

_____

_____

    2. Develop your analysis of these two documents further by answering one or two questions listed in the "Questions to Consider" section for each document.

_____

_____

_____

_____

_____

_____

_____

_____

_____

_____

_____

CHIEF JOSEPH.
NEZ PERCES.

Part Three

THE CONQUEST OF THE WEST, RECONSTRUCTION, AND THE RISE OF BIG BUSINESS

Document Seventeen

Frederick Jackson Turner Outlines the "Frontier Thesis"

Context: *In 1893, Frederick Jackson Turner was a young historian when he delivered this paper in Chicago, which was the site of a huge world's fair commemorating the 400th anniversary of Christopher Columbus and the "discovery" of the Americas. Turner's paper gradually gained renown as one of the most influential arguments in U.S. history. Keep in mind that Turner was writing in a time of tremendous economic and social change, which included mass immigration and the dramatic growth of large cities. Many of Turner's specific arguments are now dated, but his broader thesis continues to generate debate among U.S. historians.*

Questions to Consider: *What is Turner's basic argument? How does Turner define the frontier—is it a place, a process, or something altogether different? What groups did Turner ignore? Why would Turner's contemporaries find "The Significance of the Frontier" alternatively reaffirming and disturbing? What similarities and differences do you see in the ways Turner and Tocqueville conceived of the American character? Why do you think Turner's thesis has been so influential and hotly debated among historians?*

Frederick Jackson Turner, "The Significance of the Frontier in American History" (1893)

In a recent bulletin of the Superintendent of the Census for 1890 appear these significant words: "Up to and including 1880 the country had a frontier of settlement, but at present the unsettled area has been so broken into by isolated bodies of settlement that there can hardly be said to be a frontier line. In the discussion of its extent, its westward movement, etc., it can not, therefore, any longer have a place in the census reports." This brief official statement marks the closing of a great historic movement. Up to our own day American history has been in a large degree the history of the colonization of the Great West. The existence of an area of free land, its continuous recession, and the advance of American settlement westward, explain American development.

Behind institutions, behind constitutional forms and modifications, lie the vital forces that call these organs into life and shape them to meet changing conditions. The peculiarity of American institutions is, the fact that they have been compelled to adapt themselves to the changes of an expanding people—to the changes involved in crossing a continent, in winning a wilderness, and in developing at each area of this progress out of the primitive economic and political conditions of the frontier into the complexity of city life. . . . American development has exhibited not merely advance along a single line, but a return to primitive conditions on a continually advancing frontier line, and a new development for that area. American social development has been continually beginning over again on the frontier. This perennial rebirth, this fluidity of American life, this expansion westward with its new opportunities, its continuous touch with the simplicity of primitive society, furnish the forces dominating American character. The true point of view in the history of this nation is not the Atlantic coast, it is the Great West. . . .

In this advance, the frontier is the outer edge of the wave—the meeting point between savagery and civilization. . . . The most significant thing about the American frontier is, that it lies at the hither edge of free land. . . .

In the settlement of America we have to observe how European life entered the continent, and how America modified and developed that life and reacted on Europe. Our early history is the study of European germs developing in an American environment . . . The frontier is the line of most rapid and effective Americanization. The wilderness masters the colonist. It finds him a European in dress, industries, tools, modes of travel, and thought. It takes him from the railroad car and puts him in the birch canoe. It strips off the garments of civilization and arrays him in the hunting shirt and the moccasin. It puts him in the log cabin of the Cherokee and Iroquois and runs an Indian palisade around him. Before long he has gone to planting Indian corn and plowing with a sharp stick, he shouts the war cry and takes the scalp in orthodox Indian fashion. In short, at the frontier the environment is at first too strong for the man. He must accept the conditions which it furnishes, or perish, and so he fits himself into the Indian clearings and follows the Indian trails.

Little by little he transforms the wilderness, but the outcome is not the old Europe . . . The fact is, that here is a new product that is American. At first, the frontier was the Atlantic coast. It was the frontier of Europe in a very real sense. Moving westward, the frontier became more and more American. . . . Thus the advance of the frontier has meant a steady movement away from the influence of Europe, a steady growth of independence on American lines. And to study this advance, the men who grew up under these conditions, and the political, economic, and social results of it, is to study the really American part of our history. . . .

At the Atlantic frontier one can study the germs of processes repeated at each successive frontier. We have the complex European life sharply precipitated by the wilderness into the simplicity of primitive conditions. The first frontier had to meet its Indian question, its question of the disposition of the public domain, of the means of intercourse with older settlements, of the extension of political organization, of religious and educational activity. And the settlement of these and similar questions for one frontier served as a guide for the next. . . .

Why was it that the Indian trader passed so rapidly across the continent? What effects followed from the trader's frontier? . . . The explanation of the rapidity of this advance is bound up with the effects of the trade on the Indian. The trading post left the unarmed tribes at the mercy of those that had purchased firearms—a truth which the Iroquois Indians wrote in blood, and so the remote and unvisited tribes gave eager welcome to the trade. "The savages," wrote LaSalle, "take better care of us French than of their own children; from us only can they get guns and goods." This accounts for the trader's power and the rapidity of his advance. Thus the disintegrating forces of civilization entered the wilderness. Every river valley and Indian trail became a fissure in Indian society, and so that society became honeycombed. Long before the pioneer farmer appeared on the scene, primitive Indian life had passed away. . . .

The buffalo trail became the Indian trail, and this became the trader's "trace"; the trails widened into roads, and the roads into turnpikes, and these in turn were transformed into railroads. . . . Thus civilization in America has followed the arteries made by geology, pouring an ever richer tide through them, until at last the slender paths of aboriginal intercourse have been broadened and interwoven into the complex mazes of modern commercial lines; the wilderness has been interpenetrated by lines of civilization growing ever more numerous. It is like the steady growth of a complex nervous system for the originally simple, inert continent. . . .

But the most important effect of the frontier has been in the promotion of democracy here and in Europe. As has been indicated, the frontier is productive of individualism. Complex society is precipitated by the wilderness into a kind of primitive organization based on the family. The tendency is anti-social. It produces antipathy to control, and particularly to any direct control. . . . The frontier individualism has from the beginning promoted democracy. The frontier States that came into the Union in the first quarter of a century of its existence came in with democratic suffrage provisions, and had reactive effects of the highest importance upon the older States whose peoples were being attracted there. An extension of the franchise became essential. . . . The rise of democracy as an effective force in the nation came in with western preponderance under Jackson and William Henry Harrison, and it meant the triumph of the frontier—with all of its good and with all of its evil elements. . . .

So long as free land exists, the opportunity for a competency exists, and economic power secures political power. But the democracy born of free land, strong in selfishness and individualism, intolerant of administrative experience and education, and pressing individual liberty beyond its proper bounds, has its dangers as well as its benefits. Individualism in America has allowed a laxity in regard to governmental affairs which has rendered possible the spoils system and all the manifest evils that follow from the lack of a highly developed civic spirit. In this connection may be noted also the influence of frontier conditions in permitting lax business honor, inflated paper currency and wild-cat banking. . . .

The East has always feared the result of an unregulated advance of the frontier, and has tried to check and guide it. . . . But the attempts to limit the boundaries, to restrict land sales and settlement, and to deprive the West of its share of political power were all in vain. Steadily the frontier of settlement advanced and carried with it individualism, democracy, and nationalism. . .

From the conditions of frontier life came intellectual traits of profound importance. The works of travelers along each frontier from colonial days onward describe certain common traits, and these traits have, while softening down, still persisted as survivals in the place of their origin, even when a higher social organization succeeded. The result is that to the frontier the American intellect owes its striking characteristics. That coarseness and strength combined with acuteness and inquisitiveness; that practical, inventive turn of mind, quick to find expedients; that masterful grasp of material things, lacking in the artistic but powerful to effect great ends; that restless, nervous energy; that dominant individualism, working for good and for evil, and withal that buoyancy and exuberance which comes with freedom—these are traits of the frontier, or traits called out elsewhere because of the existence of the frontier. Since the days when the fleet of Columbus sailed into the waters of the New World, America has been another name for opportunity, and the people of the United States have taken their tone from the incessant expansion which has not only been open but has even been forced upon them. He would be a rash prophet who should assert that the expansive character of American life has now entirely ceased. Movement has been its dominant fact, and, unless this training has no effect upon a people, the American energy will continually demand a wider field for its exercise. But never again will such gifts of free land offer themselves. For a moment, at the frontier, the bonds of custom are broken and unrestraint is triumphant. There is not tabula rasa. The stubborn American environment is there with its imperious summons to accept its conditions; the inherited ways of doing things are also there; and yet, in spite of environment, and in spite of custom, each frontier did indeed furnish a new field of opportunity, a gate of escape from the bondage of the past; and freshness, and confidence, and scorn of older society, impatience of its restraints and its ideas, and indifference to its lessons, have accompanied the frontier. . . . And now, four centuries from the discovery of America, at the end of a hundred years of life under the Constitution, the frontier has gone, and with its going has closed the first period of American history.

Document Eighteen

J. Q. Smith Proposes New Indian Policy

Context: *J. Q. Smith was the Indian Commissioner in 1876, when he wrote this report to the Secretary of the Interior. In 1877, federal troops under Philip Sheridan crushed a Sioux-Cheyenne uprising in the Dakotas, which spelled the end of Indian military resistance throughout much of the West. After the military subjugation of the western Indians, a reform movement to "civilize" Native Americans gained momentum among some white middle-class Protestants. A major goal of the reform movement was to give land to individual families and end tribal ownership. In 1887, the Dawes Act allotted land directly to Indian families—just as Smith proposed in this plan—but much of the land ended up in the hands of white settlers.*

Questions to Consider: *What problems did Smith see in Indian policy as it stood in 1876? How did he define "civilization?" Did Smith genuinely care for the welfare of Native Americans? In what ways were his proposals constructive? In what ways were they misguided? How did Smith characterize previous Indian Removals? Why did Smith refer to Reconstruction policies in the South? Why did Smith assume the extinction of Americans Indians to be "inevitable"?*

"Report of J. Q. Smith to the Secretary of Interior" (1876)

From the first settlement of the country by white men until a comparatively recent period, the Indians have been constantly driven westward from the Atlantic. A zigzag, ever-varying line, more or less definitely marked, extending from Canada to the Gulf of Mexico, and always slowly moving west, has been known as the "frontier" or "border." Along this border has been an almost incessant struggle, the Indians to retain and the whites to get possession; the war being broken by periods of occasional and temporary peace, which usually followed treaties whereby the Indians agreed to surrender large tracts of their lands. This peace would continue until the lands surrendered had been occupied by whites, when the pressure of emigration would again break over the border, and the Indian, by force or treaty, be compelled to surrender another portion of his cherished hunting-grounds.

So long as the illimitable West offered to the Indian fresh hunting-grounds, he was unwilling to exchange his wild freedom and indolent existence for the restraints and toil of the rude and imperfect civilization to which it was possible for him in only one life-time to attain. If any tribe of Indians in this country had made the effort to abandon their savage mode of life, and undertake self-support by labor, it is at least doubtful whether for many years the change would not have rendered them more miserable and wretched. Their lack of means, of knowledge, and of previous training would, in all probability, have made such an attempt a conspicuous failure. If individual Indians had succeeded in acquiring property, they would probably have been swindled out of it by unscrupulous white men. The natural and the easiest course was to remove west and continue to hunt.

Toward the close of the first half of this century the tide of emigration and adventure swept even the frontier away and rushed across the continent. Throughout the vast regions of the West the adventurous, grasping Anglo-Saxon race is dominant and in possession of the fairest and richest portions of the land. Except in the Indian Territory and perhaps Dakota, the white exceeds the Indian population. No new hunting-grounds remain, and the civilization or the utter destruction of the Indians is inevitable. The next twenty-five years are to determine the fate of a race. If they cannot be taught, and taught very soon, to accept the necessities of their situation and begin in earnest to provide for their own wants by labor in civilized pursuits, they are destined to speedy extinction. From the fact that for so long a period Indian civilization has been retarded, it must not be concluded that some inherent characteristic in the race disqualifies it for civilized life. It may well be doubted whether this be true of any race of men. Surely it cannot be true of a race, any portion of which has made the actual progress realized by some of our Indians. They can and do learn to labor; they can and do learn to read. Many thousands today are engaged in civilized occupations. But the road out of barbarism is a long and difficult one. Even in enlightened Europe there are millions of people whose ancestors a few generations ago were as ignorant and poor and degraded as our most advanced Indian tribes now are. Civilization is a vague, indefinite, comparative term. Our children's grandchildren may look upon our civilization as very rude and imperfect. It is not my wish to give any rose-colored view of the present condition of our Indians. Many of them are as miserable and degraded as men can be; but it cannot be denied that others are making reasonably satisfactory progress.

Within a few years the Government has undertaken somewhat systematically to bring them into civilized life. The "peace policy" has sought to throw around them healthful associations; to place at the several agencies agents and employees of good moral and Christian character and of active sympathies; and an earnest effort has been made to teach Indians to labor and to read. It is too soon, perhaps, to assert that this effort has proved a success, but the accompanying reports of agents abundantly show that notwithstanding all surrounding difficulties, much has been accomplished toward establishing and maintaining peace, toward protecting Indians from evil influences, and toward awakening in them the desire for a better mode of life. The success of some of our agents, who have labored under reasonably favorable circumstances, deserves all praise, and has fully equaled the fondest hopes of the friends of the peace policy. Certainly enough improvement has been made to justify the continuance of the present benevolent efforts.

In considering whether modifications of existing methods may not be desirable, I have arrived at the conviction that the welfare and progress of the Indians require the adoption of three principles of policy:

> First. Concentration of all Indians on a few reservations.
>
> Second. Allotment to them of lands in severalty.
>
> Third. Extension over them of United States law and the jurisdiction of United States courts.

Consolidation of Reservations

The reservations upon which, in my opinion, the Indians should be, consolidated, are the Indian Territory (in Oklahoma), the White Earth reservation in Northern Minnesota, and a reservation in the southern part of Washington Territory, probably the Yakama reservation. . . .

I am well aware that it will take a long time, much patient effort, and considerable expense, to effect this proposed consolidation; but after consulting with many gentlemen thoroughly acquainted with Indian questions and Indian character, I am satisfied that the undertaking can be accomplished. . . .

Many of these Indians are now located on lands utterly unfit for cultivation, where starvation or perpetual support by the Government are the only alternatives. It is doubtful whether even white people could cultivate profitably the greater part of the Sioux reservation in Dakota. In the Indian Territory, on the other hand, are fertile land, a genial climate, and room for more Indians than there are in the whole Union.

That the Indian sentiment is opposed to such removal is true. Difficulties were experienced in bringing to the Territory its present inhabitants from east of the Mississippi; but the obstacles were overcome, and experience shows that there the race can thrive. With a fair degree of persistence the removal thither of other Indians can also be secured. The Pawnees have recently gone there, and seem content with their new home. The Poncas, and even the Red Cloud and Spotted Tail Sioux, give evidence that they are ready for the change; and if Congress will make a liberal appropriation to effect the removal of these Sioux, it is quite likely that within a year or two, other bands now on the Missouri River may also be induced to remove. If the Sioux are given a suitable reservation in that Territory for a permanent home, and are aided by the Government for a few years in their efforts at agriculture and stock raising, I know of no reason why they may not, in one generation, become as far advanced as are the Cherokees and Choctaws now.

The importance of reducing the number of reservations is shown by the following considerations. Many of the present reserves are almost worthless for agricultural purposes; others are rich in soil, mineral wealth, and timber. Nearly all are too small to subsist the Indians by hunting, and too large for them to occupy in agricultural and civilized pursuits. Many are so remote and difficult of access, that needed supplies can be furnished only at great expense. Nearly all are surrounded by white settlers, more or less numerous. Wherever an Indian reservation has on it good land, or timber, or minerals, the cupidity of the white man is excited, and a constant struggle is inaugurated to dispossess the Indian, in which the avarice and determination of the white man usually prevails. The length of the boundary-line between the reservations and the contiguous white settlements amounts in the aggregate to thousands of miles, every mile being a point of contact and difficulty. This aggregate boundary is so extensive as to render almost impossible the prevention of illicit trade in arms and whisky. As now constituted, these reservations are a refuge to the most lawless and desperate white men in America. There the vagabonds, the outcasts, the criminals, the most immoral and licentious of the population of the western portion of the country take up their abode, because there they are practically beyond the reach and operation of law, and can live lives of crime and debauchery with impunity and without reproach. Such men seriously obstruct, if they do not render nugatory, every effort to give assistance to the Indians.

By the concentration of Indians on a few reservations, it is obvious that much of the difficulty now surrounding the Indian question will vanish. Many agencies now conducted at large expense could be abolished. The aggregate boundary-lines between the reservations and country occupied by white people would be greatly reduced, and the danger of violence, bloodshed, and mutual wrong materially lessened. The sale of liquors and arms could be more effectually prevented; bad white men could more easily be kept out of the Indian country; necessary supplies could be more cheaply furnished; a far smaller military force would be required to keep the peace; and generally, the Indians, being more compact, could be more efficiently aided and controlled by the officers of the Government. Moreover, large bodies of land would be thrown open to settlement, proceeds of whose sale would be ample to defray all expense of the removals.

Allotments in Severalty

It is doubtful whether any high degree of civilization is possible without individual ownership of land. The records of the past and the experience of the present testify that the soil should be made secure to the individual by all the guarantees which law can devise, and that nothing less will induce men to put forth their best exertions. No general law exists which provides that Indians shall select allotments in severalty, and it seems to me a matter of great moment that provision should be made not only permitting, but requiring, the head of each Indian family, to accept the allotment of a reasonable amount of land, to be the property of himself and his lawful heirs, in lieu of any interest in any common tribal possession. Such allotments should be inalienable for at least twenty, perhaps fifty years, and if situated in a permanent Indian reservation, should be transferable only among Indians.

I am not unaware that this proposition will meet with strenuous opposition from the Indians themselves. Like the whites, they have ambitious men, who will resist to the utmost of their power any change tending to reduce the authority which they have acquired by personal effort or by inheritance; but it is essential that these men and their claims should be pushed aside and that each individual should feel that his home is his own; that he owes no allegiance to any great man or to any faction; that he has a direct personal interest in the soil on which he lives, and that that interest will be faithfully protected for him and for his children by the Government.

Law for Indians

My predecessors have frequently called attention to the startling fact that we have within our midst 275,000 people, the least intelligent portion of our population, for whom we provide no law, either for their protection or for the punishment of crime committed among themselves. Civilization even among white men could not long exist without the guarantees which law alone affords; yet our Indians are remitted by a great civilized government to the control, if control it can be called, of the rude regulations of petty, ignorant tribes. Year after year we expend millions of dollars for these people in the faint hope that, without law, we can civilize them. That hope has been, to a great degree, a long disappointment; and year after year we repeat the folly of the past. That the benevolent efforts and purposes of the Government have proved so largely fruitless, is, in my judgment, due more to its failure to make these people amenable to our laws than to any other cause, or to all other causes combined.

I believe it to be the duty of Congress at once to extend over Indian reservations the jurisdiction of United States courts, and to declare that each Indian in the United States shall occupy the same relation to law that a white man does. An Indian should be given to understand that no ancient custom, no tribal regulation, will shield him from just punishment for crime; and also that he will be effectually protected, by the authority and power of the Government, in his life, liberty, property, and character, as certainly as if he were a white man. There can be no doubt of the power of Congress to do this, and surely the intelligent Committees on Indian Affairs of the Senate and House can readily propose legislation which will accomplish this most desirable result. I regard this suggestion as by far the most important which I have to make in this report.

Since our Government was organized two questions, or rather two classes of questions, have transcended all others in importance and difficulty, viz, the relations of the Government and the white people to the negroes and to the Indians. The negro question has doubtless absorbed more of public attention, aroused more intense feeling, and cost our people more blood and treasure than any other question, if not all others combined. That question, it is to be hoped, is settled forever in the only way in which its settlement was possible—by the full admission of the negro to all the rights and privileges of citizenship. Next in importance comes the Indian question, and there can be no doubt that our Indian wars have cost us more than all the foreign wars in which our Government has been engaged. It is time that some solution of this whole Indian problem, decisive, satisfactory, just, and final, should be found. In my judgment it can be reached only by a process similar to that pursued with the negroes. . . .

For a hundred years the United States has been wrestling with the "Indian question," but has never had an Indian policy. The only thing yet done by the Government in regard to the Indians which seems to have been permanent and far-reaching in its scope and purpose, is the dedication of the Indian Territory as the final home for the race. Surely it is time that a policy should be determined on, which shall be fully understood by the Government, the people, and the Indians. We cannot afford to allow this race to perish without making an honest effort to save it. We cannot afford to keep them in our midst as vagabonds and paupers.

I appeal to the statesmen of the country to give to this subject their earnest attention; the sooner it is settled on some wise and comprehensive principle the better for all concerned. We have despoiled the Indians of their rich hunting-grounds, thereby depriving them of their ancient means of support. Ought we not and shall we not give them at least a secure home, and the cheap but priceless benefit of just and equitable laws?

Chief Joseph Speaks for His People

Context: *Much like the Cherokees, the Nez Percé tribe of eastern Oregon had cultivated good relations with white settlers. In 1855, the Nez Percé agreed to live on a large reservation that stretched from western Idaho to eastern Oregon. When gold was discovered on their lands in 1863, government officials tried to remove the Nez Percé to a far smaller reservation. The tribe resisted, and, in 1877, Chief Joseph and his band of 700 (including many women and children) held off some 2,000 soldiers for months during a 1,400 mile march through Oregon, Idaho, Wyoming, and Montana. Although finally captured in October 1877, the exploits of the Nez Percé made Chief Joseph famous. His fame, though, did little good for his tribe. Many of the Nez Percé were eventually forced to move to Indian Territory (present-day Oklahoma), where many died of disease.*

Questions to Consider: *What were the problems that the Nez Percé faced when trying to live peacefully with whites? What conditions eventually forced Chief Joseph to surrender in 1877? What are the major cultural differences, according to Chief Joseph, between whites and Indians? In what ways did Chief Joseph disagree with J. Q. Smith? In what ways did the two agree? How did the reform agenda of Chief Joseph differ from that of Frederick Douglass?*

The Writings of Chief Joseph

I.

The first white men of your people who came to our country were named Lewis and Clark. They brought many things which our people had never seen. They talked straight and our people gave them a great feast as proof that their hearts were friendly. They made presents to our chiefs and our people made presents to them. We had a great many horses of which we gave them what they needed, and they gave us guns and tobacco in return. All the Nez Perce made friends with Lewis and Clark and agreed to let them pass through their country and never to make war on white men. This promise the Nez Perce have never broken.

II.

For a short time we lived quietly. But this could not last. White men had found gold in the mountains around the land of the Winding Water. They stole a great many horses from us and we could not get them back because we were Indians. The white men told lies for each other. They drove off a great many of our cattle. Some white men branded our young cattle so they could claim them. We had no friends who would plead our cause before the law councils. It seemed to me that some of the white men in Wallowa were doing these things on purpose to get up a war. They knew we were not strong enough to fight them. I labored hard to avoid trouble and bloodshed. We gave up some of our country to the white men, thinking that then we could have peace. We were mistaken. The white men would not let us alone. We could have avenged our wrongs many times, but we did not. Whenever the Government has asked for help against other Indians we have never refused. When the white men were few and we were strong we could have killed them off, but the Nez Perce wishes to live at peace.

On account of the treaty made by the other bands of the Nez Perce the white man claimed my lands. We were troubled with white men crowding over the line. Some of them were good men, and we lived on peaceful terms with them, but they were not all good. Nearly every year the agent came over from Lapwai and ordered us to the reservation. We always replied that we were satisfied to live in Wallowa. We were careful to refuse the presents or annuities which he offered.

Through all the years since the white man came to Wallowa we have been threatened and taunted by them and the treaty Nez Perce. They have given us no rest. We have had a few good friends among the white men, and they have always advised my people to bear these taunts without fighting. Our young men are quick tempered and I have had great trouble in keeping them from doing rash things. I have carried a heavy load on my back ever since I was a boy. I learned then that we were but few while the white men were many, and that we could not hold our own with them. We were like deer. They were like grizzly bears. We had a small country. Their country was large. We were contented to let things remain as the Great Spirit Chief made them. They were not; and would change the mountains and rivers if they did not suit them.

III.

[At his surrender in the Bear Paw Mountains, 1877]

Tell General Howard that I know his heart. What he told me before I have in my heart. I am tired of fighting. Our chiefs are killed. Looking Glass is dead, Tu-hul-hil-sote is dead. The old men are all dead. It is the young men who now say yes or no. He who led the young men [Joseph's brother Alikut] is dead. It is cold and we have no blankets. The little children are freezing to death. My people—some of them have run away to the hills and have no blankets and no food. No one knows where they are—perhaps freezing to death. I want to have time to look for my children and see how many of them I can find. Maybe I shall find them among the dead. Hear me, my chiefs; my heart is sick and sad. From where the sun now stands I will fight no more against the white man.

IV.

[On a visit to Washington, D.C., 1879]

At last I was granted permission to come to Washington and bring my friend Yellow Bull and our interpreter with me. I am glad I came. I have shaken hands with a good many friends, but there are some things I want to know which no one seems able to explain. I cannot understand how the Government sends a man out to fight us, as it did General Miles, and then breaks his word. Such a government has something wrong about it. I cannot understand why so many chiefs are allowed to talk so many different ways, and promise so many different things. I have seen the Great Father Chief [President Hayes]; the Next Great Chief [Secretary of the Interior]; the Commissioner Chief; the Law Chief; and many other law chiefs [Congressmen] and they all say they are my friends, and that I shall have justice, but while all their mouths talk right I do not understand why nothing is done for my people. I have heard talk and talk but nothing is done. Good words do not last long unless they amount to something. Words do not pay for my dead people. They do not pay for my country now overrun by white men. They do not protect my father's grave. They do not pay for my horses and cattle. Good words do not give me back my children. Good words will not make good the promise of your war chief, General Miles. Good words will not give my people a home where they can live in peace and take care of themselves. I am tired of talk that comes to nothing. It makes my heart sick when I remember all the good words and all the broken promises. There has been too much talking by men who had no right to talk. Too many misinterpretations have been made; too many misunderstandings have come up between the white men and the Indians. If the white man wants to live in peace with the Indian he can live in peace. There need be no trouble. Treat all men alike. Give them the same laws. Give them all an even chance to live and grow. All men were made by the same Great Spirit Chief. They are all brothers. The earth is the mother of all people, and all people should have equal rights upon it. You might as well expect all rivers to run backward as that any man who was born a free man should be contented penned up and denied liberty to go where he pleases. If you tie a horse to a stake, do you expect he will grow fat? If you pen an Indian up on a small spot of earth and compel him to stay there, he will not be contented nor will he grow and prosper. I have asked some of the Great White Chiefs where they get their authority to say to the Indian that he shall stay in one place, while he sees white men going where they please. They cannot tell me.

I only ask of the Government to be treated as all other men are treated. If I cannot go to my own home, let me have a home in a country where my people will not die so fast. I would like to go to Bitter Root Valley. There my people would be happy; where they are now they are dying. Three have died since I left my camp to come to Washington.

When I think of our condition, my heart is heavy. I see men of my own race treated as outlaws and driven from country to country, or shot down like animals.

I know that my race must change. We cannot hold our own with the white men as we are. We only ask an even chance to live as other men live. We ask to be recognized as men. We ask that the same law shall work alike on all men. If an Indian breaks the law, punish him by the law. If a white man breaks the law, punish him also.

Let me be a free man, free to travel, free to stop, free to work, free to trade where I choose, free to choose my own teachers, free to follow the religion of my fathers, free to talk, think and act for myself—and I will obey every law or submit to the penalty.

Whenever the white man treats the Indian as they treat each other then we shall have no more wars. We shall be all alike—brothers of one father and mother, with one sky above us and one country around us and one government for all. Then the Great Spirit Chief who rules above will smile upon this land and send rain to wash out the bloody spots made by brothers' hands upon the face of the earth. For this time the Indian race is waiting and praying. I hope no more groans of wounded men and women will ever go to the ear of the Great Spirit Chief above, and that all people may be one people.

Hin-mah-too-yah-lat-kekht has spoken for his people.

Document Twenty

Homesteads for Freedmen

Context: *On January 16, 1865, General William T. Sherman issued an order promising home-steads to the former slaves who had lived and labored on the Sea Islands and rice plantations that lined the South Atlantic Coast. Sherman's order granted the settlers "possessory title" to tracts of up to forty acres until Congress could rule on the validity of their claims. On October 19, General O. O. Howard, the Freedmen's Bureau commissioner, informed the freedpeople of President Andrew Johnson's decision to restore the land to its former owners. In the correspondence below, the freedmen pleaded first with General Howard and then with President John-son to rescind the decision. While the freedmen received a sympathetic hearing from Howard, who in separate correspondence with Secretary of War Edwin Stanton confided, "something must be done to give these people and others the prospect of homesteads," President Johnson did not reverse his position. As you will see below, the handwritten letters from the three-member Committee of Freedmen contain the idiosyncratic punctuation and capitalization that typified nineteenth-century correspondence.*

Questions to Consider: *Why did the freedmen view land ownership as superior to wage labor and why did they see Johnson's decision as a betrayal? In what ways was the Committee of Freedmen's vision of freedom and assessment of race relations similar to and different from that of Frederick Douglass and Chief Joseph? How might historians use the correspondence below, including General Howard's reply to the freedmen, to illuminate Reconstruction's radical poten-tial and to explain why it failed to fulfill black dreams of liberty?*

Committee of Freedmen on Edisto Island, South Carolina, to the Freedmen's Bureau Commissioner

[Edisto Island, S.C., October 20 or 21, 1865]

General It Is with painfull Hearts that we the committe address you, we Have thorougholy considered the order which you wished us to Sighn, we wish we could do so but cannot feel our rights Safe If we do so,

General we want Homestead's; we were promised Homestead's by the government, If It does not carry out the promises Its agents made to us, If the government Haveing concluded to befriend Its late enemies and to neglect to observe the principles of common faith between

Its self and us Its allies In the war you said was over, now takes away from them all right to the soil they stand upon save such as they can get by again working for *your* late and thier *all time ememies.*—If the government does so we are left In a more unpleasant condition than our former

we are at the mercy of those who are combined to prevent us from getting land enough to lay our Fathers bones upon. We Have property In Horses, cattle, carriages, & articles of furniture, but we are landless and Homeless, from the Homes we Have lived In In the past we can only do one of three things Step Into the public *road or the sea* or remain on them working as In former time and subject to thire will as then. We can not resist It In any way without being driven out Homeless upon the road.

You will see this Is not the condition of really freemen

You ask us to forgive the land owners of our Island, *You* only lost your right arm. In war and might forgive them. The man who tied me to a tree & gave me 39 lashes & who stripped and flogged my mother & my sister & who will not let me stay In His empty Hut except I will do His planting & be Satisfied with His price & who combines with others to keep away land from me well knowing I would not Have any thing to do with Him If I Had land of my own.—that man, I cannot well forgive. Does It look as If He Has forgiven me, seeing How He tries to keep me In a condition of Helplessness

General, we cannot remain Here In such condition and If the government permits them to come back we ask It to Help us to reach land where we shall not be slaves nor compelled to work for those who would treat us as such

we Have not been treacherous, we Have not for selfish motives allied to us those who suffered like us from a common enemy & then Haveing gained *our* purpose left our allies In thier Hands There Is no rights secured to us there Is no law likely to be made which our Hands can reach. The state will make laws that we shall not be able to Hold land even If we pay for It Landless, Homeless. Voteless. we can only pray to god & Hope for *His Help, your Infuence & assistance* With consideration of esteem your Obt Servts

In behalf of the people

      Henry Bram

Committe   Ishmael Moutrie

      Yates Sampson

The Commissioner's Reply to the Freedmen

Charleston. S.C. Oct 22, 1865.

Messrs. I have just received your letter. You are right *in wanting homesteads* and will *surely be defended in the possession of every* one which you shall purchase or have already purchased. The Government does not wish to befriend its enemies and injure its friends, but considers a forgiven man in the light of a citizen restored to rights of property excepting as to slaves. The Supervisory Board must not permit what you fear. The old master would be very foolish to try a system of oppression as it would ruin them forever now that you are free. If the planters combine as you think, they will soon be able to get no labor. Their whipping post of which you complain is abolished forever. The duty of forgiveness is plain and simple. Forgive as we hope to be forgiven of Him who governs all things.

Congress must meet before any public lands can be had and before I can buy any for you. I will ask for your rights and try to obtain them. A contract may be by a lease as well as for wages, So that I do not think the Planters will object to leasing you land. Some can lease, some can buy and some can work for wages. I advise the sending to you of Northern men for Agents of the owners where true men can be found.

I think the people had better enter into contracts, leasing or for wages or purchase when possible for next year. If it dont work well something else may be tried afterwards. Send your petition to Congress, if you wish, and I will see that it is not passed by without proper attention. The President himself will urge something in your behalf.

Very Truly Yours

O. O. Howard

Letter from the Committee of Freedmen to President Johnson

Edisto Island S.C. Oct 28th 1865.

We the freedmen Of Edisto Island South Carolina have learned From you through Major General O O Howard commissioner of the Freedmans Bureau. with deep sorrow and Painful hearts of the possibility of goverment restoring These lands to the former owners. We are well aware Of the many perplexing and trying questions that burden Your mind. and do therefore pray to god (the preserver Of all. and who has through our Late and beloved President (Lincoln) proclamation and the war made Us A free people) that he may guide you in making Your decisions. and give you that wisdom that Cometh from above to settle these great and Important Questions for the best interests of the country and the Colored race: Here is where secession was born and Nurtured Here is were we have toiled nearly all Our lives as slaves and were treated like dumb Driven cattle, This is our home, we have made These lands what they are. we were the only true and Loyal people that were found in posession of these Lands. we have been always ready to strike for Liberty and humanity yea to fight if needs be To preserve this glorious union. Shall not we who Are freedman and have been always true to this Union have the same rights as are enjoyed by Others? Have we broken any Law of these United States? Have we forfieted our rights of property In Land?—If not then! are not our rights as A free people and good citizens of these United States To be considered before the rights of those who were Found in rebellion against this good and just Goverment (and now being conquered) come (as they Seem) with penitent hearts and beg forgiveness For past offences and also ask if thier lands Cannot be restored to them are these rebellious Spirits to be reinstated in thier *possessions* And we who have been abused and oppressed For many long years not to be allowed the Privilige of purchasing land But be subject To the will of these large Land owners? God fobid, Land monopoly is injurious to the advancement of the course of freedom, and if government Does not make some provision by which we as Freedmen can obtain A Homestead, we have Not bettered our condition.

We have been encouraged by government to take up these lands in small tracts, receiving Certificates of the same—we have thus far Taken Sixteen thousand (16000) acres of Land here on This Island. We are ready to pay for this land When Government calls for it. and now after What has been done will the good and just government take from us all this right and make us Subject to the will of those who have cheated and Oppressed us for many years God Forbid! We the freedmen of this Island and of the State of South Carolina—Do therefore petition to you as the President of these United States, that some provisions be made by which Every colored man can purchase land. and Hold it as his own. We wish to have A home if It be but A few acres. without some provision is Made our future is sad to look upon. yes our Situation is dangerous. we therefore look to you In this trying hour as A true friend of the poor and Neglected race. for protection and Equal Rights. with the privilege of purchasing A Homestead—A Homestead right here in the Heart of South Carolina.

We pray that god will direct your heart in Making such provision for us as freedmen which Will tend to unite these states together stronger Than ever before—May God bless you in the Administration of your duties as the President Of these United States is the humble prayer Of us all.—

In behalf of the Freedmen

Henry Bram

Committee   Ishmael. Moultrie.

Yates. Sampson.

Name: _____ Date: _____

Document Analysis Worksheet

   1. Date/Author of Document/Author's Position: Intended Audience:

   2. Why was this document written? List three points the author made that you find important.

   3. List two things the document tells you about life in the United States at the time it was written.

   4. Write a question to the author that the document left unanswered.

Name: _____ Date: _____

Comparative Analysis Worksheet

Choose two documents from this week's readings in which the document authors present different takes on a particular issue.

1. Identify two or three key points on which the authors agree and/or disagree.

_____

_____

_____

_____

_____

_____

2. Develop your analysis of these two documents further by answering one or two questions listed in the "Questions to Consider" section for each document.

_____

_____

_____

_____

_____

_____

_____

_____

_____

Document Twenty-One

William Graham Sumner Opposes Reform

Context: *A sociologist and economist, William Graham Sumner was an influential professor at Yale University from 1872 to 1909. Sumner, a champion of free trade and free markets, criticized government intervention as ineffectual and downright counterproductive. He equated the laws of economic competition with Darwin's theory of evolution. Just as evolution led to the survival of the fittest species, so, too, would free markets lead to the survival of the most productive and efficient capitalists and workers. Sumner's unflinching free-market philosophy sometimes made him a critic of big business. He railed against protective tariffs that the iron and steel business often favored, and also opposed land grants to powerful railroad corporations. Sumner, like Andrew Carnegie, also wrote against imperialism.*

Questions to Consider: *Why did Sumner oppose reform? Who does Sumner blame for poverty? How did Social Darwinism inform Sumner's views of society and reform? In Sumner's view, how do individuals relate to each other in modern society? What basic values did Sumner extol? What values did he criticize?*

William Graham Sumner, *What Social Classes Owe Each Other* (1907)

IT is commonly asserted that there are in the United States no classes, and any allusion to classes is resented. On the other hand, we constantly read and hear discussions of social topics in which the existence of social classes is assumed as a simple fact. "The poor," "the weak," "the laborers," are expressions which are used as if they had exact and well-understood definition. Discussions are made to bear upon the assumed rights, wrongs, and misfortunes of certain social classes; and all public speaking and writing consists, in a large measure, of the discussion of general plans for meeting the wishes of classes of people who have not been able to satisfy their own desires. These classes are sometimes discontented, and sometimes not. Sometimes they do not know that anything is amiss with them until the "friends of humanity" come to them with offers of aid. Sometimes they are discontented and envious. They do not take their achievements as a fair measure of their rights. They do not blame themselves or their parents for their lot, as compared with that of other people. Sometimes they claim that they have a right to everything of which they feel the need for their happiness on earth.

To make such a claim against God or Nature would, of course, be only to say that we claim a right to live on earth if we can. But God and Nature have ordained the chances and conditions of life on earth once for all. The case cannot be re-opened. We cannot get a revision of the laws of human life. We are absolutely shut up to the need and duty, if we would learn how to live happily, of investigating the laws of Nature, and deducing the rules of right living in the world as it is. These are very wearisome and commonplace tasks. They consist in labor and self-denial repeated over and over again in learning and doing. When the people whose claims we are considering are told to apply themselves to these tasks they become irritated and feel almost insulted. They formulate their claims as rights against society—that is, against some other men. In their view they have a right, not only to *pursue* happiness, but to *get* it; and if they fail to get it, they think they have a claim to the aid of other men—that is, to the labor and self-denial of other men—to get it for them. They find orators and poets who tell them that they have grievances, so long as they have unsatisfied desires.

Now, if there are groups of people who have a claim to other people's labor and self-denial, and if there are other people whose labor and self-denial are liable to be claimed by the first groups, then there certainly are "classes," and classes of the oldest and most vicious type. For a man who can command another man's labor and self-denial for the support of his own existence is a privileged person of the highest species conceivable on earth. Princes and paupers meet on this plane, and no other men are on it at all. On the other hand, a man whose labor and self-denial may be diverted from his maintenance to that of some other man is not a free man, and approaches more or less toward the position of a slave. . . . We shall find that all the schemes for producing equality and obliterating the organization of society produce a new differentiation based on the worst possible distinction—the right to claim and the duty to give one man's effort for another man's satisfaction. We shall find that every effort to realize equality necessitates a sacrifice of liberty.

Certain ills belong to the hardships of human life. They are natural. They are part of the struggle with Nature for existence. We cannot blame our fellow-men for our share of these. My neighbor and I are both struggling to free ourselves from these ills. The fact that my neighbor has succeeded in this struggle better than I constitutes no grievance for me. Certain other ills are due to the malice of men, and to the imperfections or errors of civil institutions. These ills are an object of agitation, and a subject of discussion. The former class of ills is to be met only by manly effort and energy; the latter may be corrected by associated effort. . . . The distinction here made between the ills which belong to the struggle for existence and those which are due to the faults of human institutions is of prime importance.

There is no possible definition of "a poor man." A pauper is a person who cannot earn his living; whose producing powers have fallen positively below his necessary consumption; who cannot, therefore, pay his way. A human society needs the active co-operation and productive energy of every person in it. A man who is present as a consumer, yet who does not contribute either by land, labor, or capital to the work of society, is a burden. On no sound political theory ought such a person to share in the political power of the State. He drops out of the ranks of workers and producers. Society must support him. It accepts the burden, but he must be cancelled from the ranks of the rulers likewise. . . .

The humanitarians, philanthropists, and reformers, looking at the facts of life as they present themselves, find enough which is sad and unpromising in the condition of many members of society. They see wealth and poverty side by side. They note great inequality of social position and social chances. They eagerly set about the attempt to account for what they see, and to devise schemes for remedying what they do not like. In their eagerness to recommend the less fortunate classes to pity and consideration they forget all about the rights of other classes; they gloss over all the faults of the classes in question and they exaggerate their misfortunes and their virtues. They invent new theories of property, distorting rights and perpetrating injustice, as any one is sure to do who sets about the re-adjustment of social relations with the interests of one group distinctly before his mind, and the interests of all other groups thrown into the background. When I have read certain of these discussions I have thought that it must be quite disreputable to be respectable, quite dishonest to own property, quite unjust to go one's own way and earn one's own living, and that the only really admirable person was the good-for-nothing. The man who by his own effort raises himself above poverty appears, in these discussions, to be of no account. The man who has done nothing to raise himself above poverty finds that the social doctors flock about him, bringing the capital which they have collected from the other class, and promising him the aid of the State to give him what the other had to work for. In all these schemes and projects the organized intervention of society through the State is either planned or hoped for, and the State is thus made to become the protector and guardian of certain classes. . . .

Here it may suffice to observe that, on the theories of the social philosophers to whom I have referred, we should get a new maxim of judicious living: Poverty is the best policy. If you get wealth, you will have to support other people; if you do not get wealth, it will be the duty of other people to support you.

No doubt one chief reason for the unclear and contradictory theories of class relations lies in the fact that our society, largely controlled in all its organization by one set of doctrines, still contains survivals of old social theories. In the Middle Ages men were united by custom and prescription into associations, ranks, guilds, and communities of various kinds. These ties endured as long as life lasted. Consequently society was dependent, throughout all its details, on status, and the tie, or bond, was sentimental. In our modern state, and in the United States more than anywhere else, the social structure is based on contract, and status is of the least importance. Contract, however, is rational—even rationalistic. It is also realistic, cold, and matter-of-fact. A contract relation is based on a sufficient reason, not on custom or prescription. It is not permanent. It endures only so long as the reason for it endures. In a state based on contract sentiment is out of place in any public or common affairs. It is relegated to the sphere of private and personal relations, where it depends not at all on class types, but on personal acquaintance and personal estimates. The sentimentalists among us always seize upon the survivals of the old order. They want to save them and restore them.

Whether social philosophers think it desirable or not, it is out of the question to go back to status or to the sentimental relations which once united baron and retainer, master and servant, teacher and pupil, comrade and comrade. That we have lost some grace and elegance is undeniable. That life once held more poetry and romance is true enough. But it seems impossible that any one who has studied the matter should doubt that we have gained immeasurably, and that our farther gains lie in going forward, not in going backward. The feudal ties can never be restored. If they could be restored they would bring back personal caprice, favoritism, sycophancy, and intrigue. A society based on contract is a society of free and independent men, who form ties without favor or obligation, and cooperate without cringing or intrigue. A society based on contract, therefore, gives the utmost room and chance for individual development, and for all the self-reliance and dignity of a free man. . . . a society of free men, co-operating under contract, is by far the strongest society which has ever yet existed; that no such society has ever yet developed the full measure of strength of which it is capable; and that the only social improvements which are now conceivable lie in the direction of more complete realization of a society of free men united by contract, are points which cannot be controverted. It follows, however, that one man, in a free state, cannot claim help from, and cannot be charged to give help to, another. . . .

Document Twenty-Two

Andrew Carnegie Defends the Accumulation of Wealth

Context: *The son of poor Scottish immigrants, Andrew Carnegie began his business career as a telegraph operator for the Pennsylvania Railroad. After rapidly rising through the ranks of the railroad company and acquiring a substantial fortune, he turned to the business of making steel. Technological and managerial innovations allowed Carnegie to achieve substantial economies of scale and dominate the market. When Carnegie sold his steel interests in 1901, he became one of the richest men in the world. Carnegie donated most of his vast fortune to various philanthropic causes, including the pursuit of world peace.*

Questions to Consider: *How did Carnegie defend the rise of big business and the inequality that accompanied it? What, in Carnegie's view, did the rich owe the poor? Why did Carnegie support some types of charities and oppose others? Why did Carnegie believe that individual businessmen should exert tight control over their philanthropic endeavors? How might Abraham Lincoln and other supporters of free-labor ideology have reacted to this document?*

Andrew Carnegie, "Wealth" (1889)

The problem of our age is the proper administration of wealth, so that the ties of brotherhood may still bind together the rich and poor in harmonious relationship. The conditions of human life have not only been changed, but revolutionized, within the past few hundred years. In former days there was little difference between the swelling, dress, food, and environment of the chief and those of his retainers. . . . The contrast between the palace of the millionaire and the cottage of the laborer with us to-day measures the change which has come with civilization.

This change, however, is not to be deplored, but welcomed as highly beneficial. It is well, nay, essential for the progress of the race that the houses of some should be homes for all that is highest and best in literature and the arts, and for all the refinements of civilization, rather than that none should be so. Much better this great irregularity than universal squalor. . . . The "good old times" were not good old times. Neither master nor servant was as well situated then as today. A relapse to old conditions would be disastrous to both—not the least so to him who serves—and would sweep away civilization with it. But whether the change be for good or ill, it is upon us, beyond our power to alter, and therefore to be accepted and made the best of. It is waste of time to criticize the inevitable.

It is easy to see how the change has come. . . . Formerly articles were manufactured at the domestic hearth or in small shops which formed part of the household. The master and his apprentices worked side by side, the latter living with the master, and therefore subject to the same conditions. When these apprentices rose to be masters, there was little or no change in their mode of life, and they, in turn, educated in the same routine succeeding apprentices. There was, substantially, social equality, and even political equality, for those engaged in industrial pursuits had then little or no political voice in the State.

But the inevitable result of such a mode of manufacture was crude articles at high prices. Today the world obtains commodities of excellent quality at prices which even the generation preceding this would have deemed incredible. In the commercial world similar causes have produced similar results, and the race is benefited thereby. The poor enjoy what the rich could not before afford. What were the luxuries have become the necessaries of life. The laborer has now more comforts than the farmer had a few generations ago. The farmer has more luxuries than the landlord had, and is more richly clad and better housed. The landlord has books and pictures rarer, and appointments more artistic, than the King could then obtain.

The price we pay for this salutary change is, no doubt, great. We assemble thousands of operatives in the factory, in the mine, and in the counting-house, of whom the employer can know little or nothing, and to whom the employer is little better than a myth. All intercourse between them is at an end. Rigid Castes are formed, and, as, usual, mutual ignorance breeds mutual distrust. Each Caste is without sympathy for the other, and ready to credit anything disparaging in regard to it. Under the law of competition, the employer of thousands is forced into the strictest economies, among which the rates paid to labor figure prominently, and often there is friction between the employer and the employed, between capital and labor, between rich and poor. Human society loses homogeneity.

The price which society pays for the law of competition, like the price it pays for cheap comforts and luxuries, is also great; but the advantages of this law are also greater still, for it is to this law that we owe our wonderful material development, which brings improved conditions in its train. But, whether the law be benign or not, . . . it is here; we cannot evade it; no substitutes for it have been found; and while the law may be sometimes hard for the individual, it is best for the race, because it insures the survival of the fittest in every department. We accept and welcome, therefore, as conditions to which we must accommodate ourselves, great inequality of environment, the concentration of business, industrial and commercial, in the hands of a few, and the law of competition between these, as being not only beneficial, but essential for the future progress of the race. Having accepted these, it follows that there must be great scope for the exercise of special ability in the merchant and in the manufacturer who has to conduct affairs upon a great scale, That this talent for organization and management is rare among men is proved by the fact that it invariably secures for its possessor enormous rewards, no matter where or under what laws or conditions. . . . It is a law, as certain as any of the others named, that men possessed of this peculiar talent for affairs, under the free play of economic forces, must, of necessity, soon be in receipt of more revenue than can be judiciously expended upon themselves; and this law is as beneficial for the race as the others. . . .

The Socialist or Anarchist who seeks to overturn present conditions is to be regarded as attacking the foundation upon which civilization itself rests, for civilization took its start from the day that the capable, industrious workman said to his incompetent and lazy fellow, "If thou dost not sow, thou shalt no reap," and thus ended primitive Communism by separating the drones from the bees. One who studies this subject will soon be brought face to face with the conclusion that upon the sacredness of property civilization itself depends—the right of the laborer to his hundred dollars in the savings bank, and equally the legal right of the millionaire to his millions. To those who propose to substitute Communism for this intense Individualism the answer, therefore, is: The race has tried that. All progress from that barbarous day to the present time has resulted from its displacement. Not evil, but good, has come to the race from the accumulation of wealth by those who have the ability and energy that produce it. . . . Individualism, Private Property, the Law of Accumulation of Wealth, and the Law of Competition; these are the highest results of human experience, the soil in which society so far has produced the best fruit. Unequally or unjustly, perhaps, as these laws sometimes operate, and imperfect as they appear to the Idealist, they are, nevertheless, like the highest type of man, the best and most valuable of all that humanity has yet accomplished.

We start, then, with a condition of affairs under which the best interests of the race are promoted, but which inevitably gives wealth to the few. Thus far, accepting conditions as they exist, the situation can be surveyed and pronounced good. The question then arises, what is the proper mode of administering wealth after the laws upon which civilization is founded have thrown it into the hands of the few? . . .

There are but three modes in which surplus wealth can be disposed of. It can be left to the families of the decedents; or it can be bequeathed for public purposes; or, finally, it can be administered during their lives by its possessors. Under the first and second modes most of the wealth of the world that has reached the few has hitherto been applied. . . . Why should men leave great fortunes to their children? If this is done from affection, is it not misguided affection? Observation teaches that, generally speaking, it is not well for the children that they should be so burdened. Neither is it well for the state. Beyond providing for the wife and daughters moderate sources of income, and very moderate allowances indeed, if any, for the sons, men may well hesitate, for it is no longer questionable that great sums bequeathed oftener work more for the injury than for the good of the recipients. Wise men will soon conclude that, for the best interests of the members of their families and of the state, such bequests are an improper use of their means. . . .

As to the second mode, that of leaving wealth at death for public uses, it may be said that this is only a means for the disposal of wealth, provided a man is content to wait until he is dead before it becomes of much good in the world. Knowledge of the results of legacies bequeathed is not calculated to inspire the brightest hopes of much posthumous good being accomplished. The cases are not few in which the real object sought by the testator is not attained, nor are they few in which his real wishes are thwarted. In many cases the bequests are so used as to become only monuments of his folly. It is well to remember that it requires the exercise of not less ability than that which acquired the wealth to use it so as to be really beneficial to the community. . . .

The growing disposition to tax more and more heavily large estates left at death is a cheering indication of the growth of a salutary change in public opinion. . . . Men who continue hoarding great sums all their lives, the proper use of which for the public ends would work good to the community, should be made to feel that the community, in the form of the state, cannot thus be deprived of its proper share. By taxing estates heavily at death the state marks its condemnation of the selfish millionaire's unworthy life. . . .

There remains, then, only one mode of using great fortunes; but in this we have the true antidote for the temporary unequal distribution of wealth, the reconciliation of the rich and the poor—a reign of harmony—another ideal, differing, indeed, from that of the Communist in requiring only the further evolution of existing conditions, not the total overthrow of our civilization. It is founded upon the present most intense individualism, and the race is prepared to put it in practice by degrees whenever it pleases. Under its sway we shall have an ideal state, in which the surplus wealth of the few will become, in the best sense, the property of the many, because administered for the common good, and this wealth, passing through the hands of the few, can be made a much more potent force for the elevation of our race than if it had been distributed in small sums to the people themselves. . . .

This, then, is held to be the duty of the man of Wealth: First, to set an example of modest, unostentatious living, shunning display or extravagance; to provide moderately for the legitimate wants of those dependent upon him; and after doing so to consider all surplus revenues which come to him simply as trust funds, which he is called upon to administer, and strictly bound as a matter of duty to administer in the manner which, in his judgment, is best calculated to produce the most beneficial results for the community—the man of wealth thus becoming the mere agent and trustee for his poorer brethren, bringing to their service his superior wisdom, experience, and ability to administer, doing for them better than they would or could do for themselves. . . .

Those who would administer wisely must, indeed, be wise, for one of the serious obstacles to the improvement of our race is indiscriminate charity. It were better for mankind that the millions of the rich were thrown into the sea than so spent as to encourage the slothful, the drunken, the unworthy. . . .

In bestowing charity, the main consideration should be to help those who will help themselves; to provide part of the means by which those who desire to improve may do so; to give those who desire to rise the aids by which they may rise; to assist, but rarely or never to do all. . . . Every one has, of course, cases of individuals brought to his own knowledge where temporary assistance can do genuine good, and these he will not overlook. But the amount which can be wisely given by the individual for individuals is necessarily limited by his lack of knowledge of the circumstances connected with each. He is the only true reformer who is as careful and as anxious not to aid the unworthy as he is to aid the worthy, and, perhaps, even more so, for in aims-giving more injury is probably done by rewarding vice than by relieving virtue. . . .

Thus is the problem of Rich and Poor to be solved. The laws of accumulation will be left free; the laws of distribution free. Individualism will continue, but the millionaire will be but a trustee for the poor; entrusted for a season with a great part of the increased wealth of the community, but administering it for the community far better than it could or would have done for itself. . . . The man who dies leaving behind him millions of available wealth, which was his to administer during life, will pass away "unwept, unhonored, and unsung," no matter to what uses he leaves the dross which he cannot take with him. Of such as these the public verdict will then be: "The man who dies thus rich dies disgraced."

Such, in my opinion, is the true Gospel concerning Wealth, obedience to which is destined some day to solve the problem of the Rich and the Poor, and to bring "Peace on earth, among men Good Will."

Document Twenty-Three

Union Leaders Debate "Pure and Simple" Unionism

Context: *In the late nineteenth and early twentieth centuries, union leaders and grassroots organizers heatedly debated how workers could best respond to the growing power of corporations. Many workers belonged to the Knights of Labor, an inclusive organization that sought to abolish the "wage system." When the Knights of Labor collapsed, Samuel Gompers and the American Federation of Labor (AFL) became the most influential voice of the labor movement. Focusing on pragmatic demands for higher wages and an eight-hour day, the AFL organized mostly skilled and craft workers. The AFL strategy upset many socialists who believed that a more inclusive political approach was needed. In the first document, Adolph Strasser, a longtime ally of Gompers, defines what would become known as "Pure and Simple" unionism. In the second document, socialist Mahlon Barnes criticizes this approach as "pure and simpledom."*

Questions to Consider: *What were the ultimate goals of Strasser and his trade union? Why did Strasser emphasize the negative consequences of overproduction and how did he propose to combat them? In what ways, according to Strasser, were trade unions actually conservative institutions? Were there any radical elements to Strasser's political program? What, according to Barnes, were the weaknesses of the AFL? What political program did Barnes support? What type of worker was more likely to support Barnes instead of Strasser?*

Adolph Strasser, Congressional Testimony (1883)

Question. Please state your residence and occupation.—**Answer.** I reside in New York. At present I am acting president and secretary of the Cigarmakers' International Union of America, and editor of the journal of the organization. I do not work at my trade now, but am simply acting as an officer of the Cigarmakers' International Union. . . .

Q. I see you recognize the idea of overproduction and of the necessity of obtaining outlets for our products in order that panics may be avoided. In that line it occurs to me to ask you whether it is in contemplation, as one of the ultimate purposes of the trades unions, that their funds shall be accumulated so that if, in order to prevent a panic by the excess of products being thrown upon the market, they can in future lessen production by suspending labor for a time, and maintain the laborers meanwhile out of the accumulated fund. Have your trades organizations any such idea as that?—**A.** The trades unions try to prevent panics, but in fact they cannot prevent them, because panics are governed by influences beyond their control.

Q. Panics result, do they not, largely from overproduction?—**A.** The trades unions try to make their members better consumers, thereby enlarging the home market, and at the same time to make them better producers. If we can make the working people generally better consumers we shall have no panics.

Q. But if the increase of the power of production goes on by the improvement of machinery and all that, will no your efforts be counteracted in that way?—**A.** Then we propose a reduction of the hours of labor. That will decrease production and will increase consumption. We hold that a man who works but eight hours a day will demand a better home than a man who works longer hours; he will not be willing to live in one or two squalid rooms; he will demand better clothes, better food, more books, more newspapers, more education; more of the commodities that labor provides, more of the world's wealth, and that will bring about a better distribution of wealth and will consequently check panics to a certain extent. I do not believe that it is possible for the trades unions to do away with panics altogether, because panics depend not merely upon the condition of the industries of the United States, but upon the condition of the industries of the whole civilized world.

Q. Do you not contemplate, in the end, the participation of all labor and of all men in the benefits of the trades unions?—**A.** Of course we try to extend the good of the trades unions as well as we can and as far as we can.

By Mr. Pugh:

Q. You are seeking to improve home matters first?—**A.** Yes, sir; I look first to the trade I represent; I look first to cigars, to the interests of men who employ me to represent their interests.

The CHAIRMAN. I was only asking you in regard to your ultimate ends.

The WITNESS. We have no ultimate ends. We are going on from day to day. We are fighting only for immediate objects—objects that can be realized in a few years.

By Mr. Call:

Q. You want something better to eat and to wear, and better houses to live in?—**A.** Yes; we want to dress better and to live better, and become better off and better citizens generally.

The CHAIRMAN. I see that you are a little sensitive lest it should be thought that you are a mere theorizer. I do not look upon you in that light at all.

The WITNESS. Well, we say in our constitution that we are opposed to theorists, and I have to represent the organization here. We are all practical men.

By the Chairman:

Q. Have you not a theory upon which you have organized?—**A.** Yes, sir; our theory is the experience of the past in the United States and in Great Britain. That is our theory, based upon actual facts. Our organization has been experimenting for the last twenty years until we have arrived at a solid footing resting on experience.

Q. In other words you have arrived at the theory which you are trying to apply?—**A.** We have arrived at a practical result.

Q. But a practical result is the application of a theory, is it not?—**A.** Well, certainly there is no practical result without some theory.

Q. I agree to that. The difference is between good theories and bad ones, between false theories and true ones.—**A.** Yes; that is all.

By Mr. Pugh:

Q. You have furnished us with a very valuable fund of information. Have you any further statement to make of any other facts connected with this labor question?—**A.** Well, I have not yet proposed any remedies.

Q. We shall be glad to hear your views on that subject.

A. Well, we propose—

1. That trades unions shall be incorporated. At present there are a great many of the States that do not protect our funds. It is simply a breach of trust to use our funds improperly and we have lost considerable money in that way. . . . Being, as we are, a benevolent organization, we desire some protection from the Government, that is, a legal recognition and protection for the property we hold. The money we hold today is invested in savings banks, in probably 145 different banks, and there may be an opportunity to invest it in some safer institutions or in something else; but at present we have no right to invest our money except in Government bonds or in savings banks, and we claim the same right as the banks and other corporations have to be incorporated. . . .

2. The next demand we make, one which we think will benefit labor, is the enforcement of the eight-hour law and its extension to the operation of all patents granted by the, Government. . . .

3. Our third demand is this: We claim that it is necessary to obtain information in regard to such questions as those which this committee is now investigating, and to that end we believe there is a necessity for a national bureau of labor statistics. . . . We hold

that such a national bureau of labor statistics would give our legislators a great deal of information which will be very valuable to them as legislators, and we hold further that it would be a benefit, not only to labor, but, also, even greater benefit to capital, to have all this information compiled annually and distributed generally.

4. Our fourth demand is what I have already stated, that the Senate Committee on Finance shall report an amendment to the revenue laws, prohibiting the granting of licenses after May 4, 1884, to prisons, penitentiaries, and other such places for the manufacture of cigars. This demand is made, of course, simply in the interest of my own trade.

These are all the demands which we think it necessary to make now, and we believe that if these are granted, they will tend to relieve labor, to prevent strikes, and to accomplish the results formulated in the resolution of the Senate under which you are acting.

Q. Is the tendency of the trades unions on the whole to increase or to lessen strikes, as an ultimate result?—**A.** Our organization has prevented within the last three years over 200 strikes. No strike for an increase of wages can be approved under our constitution unless by a two-thirds vote of all the unions, and if a union makes an unreasonable demand it is voted down. . . .

Q. Do you not believe that is the tendency of trades organizations generally?—**A.** Yes; there is a tendency in old organizations to avoid strikes; new organizations are generally formed for the purpose of jumping into a strike. . . .

Q. What is the feeling on the part of wage receivers generally towards their employers; is it a feeling of amity and confidence or is it a feeling of distrust?—**A.** In places where men receive good wages there is a general good feeling; where they receive poor wages—starvation wages— there is generally bad feeling. The feeling between labor and capital depends largely on the employers. If they treat their men well and pay them fair wages, there is generally good feeling. If the employers treat their men badly and pay starvation wages, there is generally bad feeling. It depends wholly upon the employer. He has the power to encourage good feeling or the reverse.

Q. Mr. Lenz, the editor of a paper called Capital and Labor, expressed an opinion here that there was a growing socialistic feeling among the members of the trades unions; what is your observation in regard to that?—**A.** It is not so in the Cigar-makers' International Union. That organization does not inquire into the private opinions of a member; it takes in Democrats and Republicans, or anybody else so long as they are workers at the trade; that organization aims at practical measures, and will not allow any vague theories to be foisted upon it.

Q. Then you deny Mr. Lenz's statement so far as it relates to your organization?—**A.** As regards the Cigar-makers' International Union, I positively deny it. The members of that organization are simply practical men, going for practical objects that can be accomplished in a few years; they are no "trimmers."

Mahlon Barnes, "Pure and Simpledom" (1896)

And what is pure and simpledom doing to meet the changed conditions which confront us? . . . You can just about as much batter down monopoly with the boycott and wring material concessions from organized capital through strikes, with the law, the machinery of the State, and the power and armament of government on land and sea against you, as you can batter down the great granite shaft on Bunker Hill with a battering ram pointed with a pumpkin . . .

Mind you, we do not undervalue the potency of strikes nor ignore the necessity of boycotts. We Socialists are the best, the most persistent and the most uncompromising strikers and boycotters on earth. . . . But we Socialists desire to extend the power of trades unions and of the working class by uniting political action with economic resistance. We propose to use the highest intellectual weapon known to man; that which has come to us through 600 years of struggle in which the brain and brawn of Roman, Dane, Celt and Saxon and Norman was commingled, and we propose to unite the ballot with the strike and boycott.

In England and the United States trades unions preceded Socialism. Our spirit is now slowly but persistently, and I believe triumphantly, entering the body of the rank and file of organized labor. It has already done so to considerable extent in the large cities, and is gradually permeating the most alert and intelligent men and women in the ranks of labor . . .

What is all this, let me ask you in all seriousness, but the broader and more-intelligent application of trades union methods? To strike down the representatives of capitalism in the supreme law-making bodies of the world, and placing therein the representatives of organized labor is the kind of a strike that ever can be engaged in.

To refuse to vote money out of the pockets of the people to be expended for powder, bullets and guns, to make your sons bayonet-bearers and cannon-fodder, to orphan your brother and widow your sisters, to break mothers' hearts and fill the land with tears and blood so that plutocracy may survive and barbarism perpetuate itself—that is the most sublime boycott conceivable to the mind of man.

But at the exact point where old trades unionism raises the white flag, Socialism raises the red flag, and insists that there is a class struggle and that capitalism can and must be disarmed at the ballot box, where the workers outnumber its cohorts a thousand to one.

Let me point out to you the fundamental difference between this—the method of Socialism, and the methods of pure and simpledom.

We have had, upon the economic field, such reverses as came to us from Homestead, Chicago, Philadelphia, Brooklyn, Milwaukee, etc, from which even the most fossilized trades unionist cannot possibly draw more than the "sweet use of adversity." If concentration of wealth into the hands of the few necessitates the pauperization of the masses proportioned to the perfection of machinery, the reduction of wages and increased precariousness of the position of the wage earners, then it follows that the power of resistance on the part of the worker becomes constantly more feeble—defeats more certain and frequent, and victories like angel's visits, fewer and farther between. The result is the logical and necessary outcome of conditions—is certain, absolute and inevitable—and it is discouraging and disheartening to trades unionists and all who sympathize with labor.

Mark now the difference. With honest leaders who will preach the truth and labor for class-consciousness, the great lessons taught by the failures will intensify class feeling, rending more and more clearly apparent the necessity of political action, and as every election, municipal, state and national, registers the growth of class-consciousness, we shall go, instead of from defeat to defeat, like scourged hounds, from triumph to victory as our growing numbers pass in review, and as the unconquerable hosts of labor, armed with the freeman's ballot, come nearer and nearer possessing themselves of the functions of governmental power, legislative, judicial and executive.

I know very well the pure and simple leaders call us dreamers; but are you [not] quite sure that they themselves are either asleep, or blind, or both?

Dreamers! Indeed? So was Moses, marching out of plague-smitten Egypt with hope-uplifted Israel. So was Luther of Worms defying Rome in her pride of power—the noblest of all the noble there. . . . And so was [William Lloyd] Garrison, the iron-hearted, whom you have placed in magnificent bronze overlooking the Commons.

Darkness or light, justice or might, slavery or freedom, Socialism or capitalism, that is the real issue which confronts the world to-day.

Name: _____ Date: _____

Document Analysis Worksheet

1. Date/Author of Document/Author's Position: Intended Audience:

2. Why was this document written? List three points the author made that you find important.

3. List two things the document tells you about life in the United States at the time it was written.

4. Write a question to the author that the document left unanswered.

Name: _____ Date: _____

Comparative Analysis Worksheet

Choose two documents from this week's readings in which the document authors present different takes on a particular issue.

    1. Identify two or three key points on which the authors agree and/or disagree.

_____

_____

_____

_____

_____

_____

    2. Develop your analysis of these two documents further by answering one or two questions listed in the "Questions to Consider" section for each document.

_____

_____

_____

_____

_____

_____

_____

_____

_____

_____

Part Four

THE PROGRESSIVE ERA

Document Twenty-Four

Populists Put Forth Reform Agenda

Context: *Officially organized in 1892, the People's Party (better known as the Populists) was a result of widespread discontent in many farm states. Low farm prices for corn, wheat, and cotton devastated many farmers in the Great Plains states and the South. Part of the Populist solution revolved around inflationary monetary policies that would increase farm prices. The Populists also sought to limit the political influence of large-scale industrial corporations, which many farmers saw as the root of the nation's economic and political problems.*

Questions to Consider: *Some historians have argued that the Populists were backwards looking in their policies and approach. Do you agree with that assessment? In what ways did the Populists invoke the republicanism of Andrew Jackson? What types of reforms did the Populists emphasize as the most important? What grievances, strategies, and goals did the Populists share with labor unions, socialists, and progressives? What elements of the Populists agenda remain hot-button political issues even in our own day?*

National People's Party Platform (1892)

Assembled upon the 116th anniversary of the Declaration of Independence, the People's Party of America, in their first national convention, invoking upon their action the blessing of Almighty God, put forth in the name and on behalf of the people of this country, the following preamble and declaration of principles:

Preamble

The conditions which surround us best justify our co-operation; we meet in the midst of a nation brought to the verge of moral, political, and material ruin. Corruption dominates the ballot-box, the Legislatures, the Congress, and touches even the ermine of the bench. The people are demoralized; most of the States have been compelled to isolate the voters at the polling places to prevent universal intimidation and bribery. The newspapers are largely subsidized or muzzled, public opinion silenced, business prostrated, homes covered with mortgages, labor impoverished, and the land concentrating in the hands of capitalists. The urban workmen are denied the right to organize for self-protection, imported pauperized labor beats down their wages, a hireling standing army, unrecognized by our laws, is established to shoot them down, and they are rapidly degenerating into European conditions. The fruits of the toil of millions are boldly stolen to build up colossal fortunes for a few, unprecedented in the history of mankind; and the possessors of those, in turn, despise the republic and endanger liberty. From the same prolific womb of governmental injustice we breed the two great classes—tramps and millionaires.

The national power to create money is appropriated to enrich bondholders; a vast public debt payable in legal tender currency has been funded into gold-bearing bonds, thereby adding millions to the burdens of the people.

Silver, which has been accepted as coin since the dawn of history, has been demonetized to add to the purchasing power of gold by decreasing the value of all forms of property as well as human labor, and the supply of currency is purposely abridged to fatten usurers, bankrupt enterprise, and enslave industry. A vast conspiracy against mankind has been organized on two continents, and it is rapidly taking possession of the world. If not met and overthrown at once it forebodes terrible social convulsions, the destruction of civilization, or the establishment of an absolute despotism.

We have witnessed for more than a quarter of a century the struggles of the two great political parties for power and plunder, while grievous wrongs have been inflicted upon the suffering people. We charge that the controlling influences dominating both these parties have permitted the existing dreadful conditions to develop without serious effort to prevent or restrain them. Neither do they now promise us any substantial reform. They have agreed together to ignore, in the coming campaign, every issue but one. They propose to drown the outcries of a plundered people with the uproar of a sham battle over the tariff, so that capitalists, corporations, national banks, rings, trusts, watered stock, the demonetization of silver and the oppressions of the usurers may all be lost sight of. They propose to sacrifice our homes, lives, and children on the altar of mammon; to destroy the multitude in order to secure corruption funds from the millionaires.

Assembled on the anniversary of the birthday of the nation, and filled with the spirit of the grand general and chief who established our independence, we seek to restore the government of the Republic to the hands of "the plain people," with which class it originated. We assert our purposes to be identical with the purposes of the National Constitution; to form a more perfect union and establish justice, insure domestic tranquillity, provide for the common defence, promote the general welfare, and secure the blessings of liberty for ourselves and our posterity.

We declare that this Republic can only endure as a free government while built upon the love of the whole people for each other and for the nation; that it cannot be pinned together by bayonets; that the civil war is over, and that every passion and resentment which grew out of it must die with it, and that we must be in fact, as we are in name, one united brotherhood of free men.

Our country finds itself confronted by conditions for which there is no precedent in the history of the world; our annual agricultural productions amount to billions of dollars in value, which must, within a few weeks or months, be exchanged for billions of dollars' worth of commodities consumed in their production; the existing currency supply is wholly inadequate to make this exchange; the results are falling prices, the formation of combines and rings, the impoverishment of the producing class. We pledge ourselves that if given power we will labor to correct these evils by wise and reasonable legislation, in accordance with the terms of our platform.

We believe that the power of government—in other words, of the people—should be expanded (as in the case of the postal service) as rapidly and as far as the good sense of an intelligent people and the teachings of experience shall justify, to the end that oppression, injustice, and poverty shall eventually cease in the land.

While our sympathies as a party of reform are naturally upon the side of every proposition which will tend to make men intelligent, virtuous, and temperate, we nevertheless regard these questions, important as they are, as secondary to the great issues now pressing for solution, and upon which not only our individual prosperity but the very existence of free institutions depend; . . . the forces of reform this day organized will never cease to move forward until every wrong is remedied and equal rights and equal privileges securely established for all the men and women of this country.

Platform

We declare, therefore—

First.—That the union of the labor forces of the United States this day consummated shall be permanent and perpetual; may its spirit enter into all hearts for the salvation of the Republic and the uplifting of mankind.

Second.—Wealth belongs to him who creates it, and every dollar taken from industry without an equivalent is robbery. "If any will not work, neither shall he eat." The interests of rural and civic labor are the same; their enemies are identical.

Third.—We believe that the time has come when the railroad corporations will either own the people or the people must own the railroads, and should the government enter upon the work of owning and managing all railroads, we should favor an amendment to the Constitution by which all persons engaged in the government service shall be placed under a civil-service regulation of the most rigid character, so as to prevent the increase of the power of the national administration by the use of such additional government employees.

FINANCE—We demand a national currency, safe, sound, and flexible, issued by the general government only, a full legal tender for all debts, public and private, and that without the use of banking corporations, a just, equitable, and efficient means of distribution direct to the people, at a tax not to exceed 2 per cent. per annum, to be provided as set forth in the sub-treasury plan of the Farmers' Alliance, or a better system; also by payments in discharge of its obligations for public improvements.

1. We demand free and unlimited coinage of silver and gold at the present legal ratio of 16 to 1.

2. We demand that the amount of circulating medium be speedily increased to not less than $50 per capita.

3. We demand a graduated income tax.

4. We believe that the money of the country should be kept as much as possible in the hands of the people, and hence we demand that all State and national revenues shall be limited to the necessary expenses of the government, economically and honestly administered.

5. We demand that postal savings banks be established by the government for the safe deposit of the earnings of the people and to facilitate exchange.

TRANSPORTATION.—Transportation being a means of exchange and a public necessity, the government should own and operate the railroads in the interest of the people. The telegraph, telephone, like the post-office system, being a necessity for the transmission of news, should be owned and operated by the government in the interest of the people.

LAND.—The land, including all the natural sources of wealth, is the heritage of the people, and should not be monopolized for speculative purposes, and alien ownership of land should be prohibited. All land now held by railroads and other corporations in excess of their actual needs, and all lands now owned by aliens should be reclaimed by the government and held for actual settlers only.

Expression of Sentiments

Your Committee on Platform and Resolutions beg leave unanimously to report the following:

Whereas, Other questions have been presented for our consideration, we hereby submit the following, not as a part of the Platform of the People's Party, but as resolutions expressive of the sentiment of this Convention.

1. RESOLVED, That we demand a free ballot and a fair count in all elections and pledge ourselves to secure it to every legal voter without Federal Intervention, through the adoption by the States of the unperverted Australian or secret ballot system.

2. RESOLVED, That the revenue derived from a graduated income tax should be applied to the reduction of the burden of taxation now levied upon the domestic industries of this country.

3. RESOLVED, That we pledge our support to fair and liberal pensions to ex-Union soldiers and sailors.

4. RESOLVED, That we condemn the fallacy of protecting American labor under the present system, which opens our ports to the pauper and criminal classes of the world and crowds out our wage-earners; and we denounce the present ineffective laws against contract labor, and demand the further restriction of undesirable emigration.

5. RESOLVED, That we cordially sympathize with the efforts of organized workingmen to shorten the hours of labor, and demand a rigid enforcement of the existing eight-hour law on Government work, and ask that a penalty clause be added to the said law.

6. RESOLVED, That we regard the maintenance of a large standing army of mercenaries, known as the Pinkerton system, as a menace to our liberties, and we demand its abolition. . . .

7. RESOLVED, That we commend to the favorable consideration of the people and the reform press the legislative system known as the initiative and referendum.

8. RESOLVED, That we favor a constitutional provision limiting the office of President and Vice-President to one term, and providing for the election of Senators of the United States by a direct vote of the people.

9. RESOLVED, That we oppose any subsidy or national aid to any private corporation for any purpose.

10. RESOLVED, That this convention sympathizes with the Knights of Labor and their righteous contest with the tyrannical combine of clothing manufacturers of Rochester, and declare it to be a duty of all who hate tyranny and oppression to refuse to purchase the goods made by the said manufacturers, or to patronize any merchants who sell such goods.

Document Twenty-Five

Theodore Roosevelt Articulates a New Nationalism

Context: *A progressive reformer from New York, Theodore Roosevelt served as president of the United States from 1901–1909. He would later lose to Democrat Woodrow Wilson in the election of 1912. The New Nationalism speech, delivered in 1910, synthesized the various strands of Roosevelt's progressive philosophy. Roosevelt was heavily influenced by Herbert Croly, a political philosopher who advocated using Hamiltonian means (activist government) to achieve Jeffersonian ends (democratic idealism).*

Questions to Consider: *In what ways did Roosevelt's "New Nationalism" contain both conservative and liberal elements? Why would many Americans living in the era of big business find Roosevelt's message appealing? Do you agree with Roosevelt's conclusion that "good character" is an essential part of public service?*

Theodore Roosevelt "The New Nationalism" (1910)

We come here to-day to commemorate one of the epoch-making events of the long struggle for the rights of man—the long struggle for the uplift of humanity. Our country—this great republic—means nothing unless it means the triumph of a real democracy, the triumph of popular government, and, in the long run, of an economic system under which each man shall be guaranteed the opportunity to show the best that there is in him. That is why the history of America is now the central feature of the history of the world; for the world has set its face hopefully toward our democracy; and, O my fellow citizens, each one of you carries on your shoulders not only the burden of doing well for the sake of your own country, but the burden of doing well and of seeing that this nation does well for the sake of mankind.

The issue is joined, and we must fight or fail. In every wise struggle for human betterment one of the main objects, and often the only object, has been to achieve in large measure equality of opportunity. In the struggle for this great end, nations rise from barbarism to civilization, and through it people press forward from one stage of enlightenment to the next. One of the chief factors in progress is the destruction of special privilege. The essence of any struggle for healthy liberty has always been, and must always be, to take from some one man or class of men the right to enjoy power, or wealth, or position, or immunity, which has not been earned by service to his or their fellows. That is what you fought for in the Civil War, and that is what we strive for now.

At many stages in the advance of humanity, this conflict between the men who possess more than they have earned and the men who have earned more than they possess is the central condition of progress. In our day it appears as the struggle of free men to gain and hold the right of self-government as against the special interests, who twist the methods of free government into machinery for defeating the popular will. At every stage, and under all circumstances, the essence of the struggle is to equalize opportunity, destroy privilege, and give to the life and citizenship of every individual the highest possible value both to himself and to the commonwealth. That is nothing new. . . .

Practical equality of opportunity for all citizens, when we achieve it, will have two great results. First, every man will have a fair chance to make of himself all that in him lies; to reach the highest point to which his capacities, unassisted by special privilege of his own and unhampered by the special privilege of others, can carry him, and to get for himself and his family substantially what he has earned. Second, equality of opportunity means that the commonwealth will get from every citizen the highest service of which he is capable. No man who carries the burden of the special privileges of another can give to the commonwealth that service to which it is fairly entitled.

I stand for the square deal. But when I say that I am for the square deal, I mean not merely that I stand for fair play under the present rules of the game, but that I stand for having those rules changed so as to work for a more substantial equality of opportunity and of reward for equally good service. One word of warning, which, I think, is hardly necessary in Kansas. When I say I want a square deal for the poor man, I do not mean that I want a square deal for the man who remains poor because he has not got the energy to work for himself. . . .

Now, this means that our government, national and state, must be freed from the sinister influence or control of special interests. Exactly as the special interests of cotton and slavery threatened our political integrity before the Civil War, so now the great special business interests too often control and corrupt the men and methods of government for their own profit. We must drive the special interests out of politics. That is one of our tasks to-day. Every special interest is entitled to justice—full, fair, and complete, and, now, mind you, if there were any attempt by mob violence to plunder and work harm to the special interest, whatever it may be, that I most dislike, and the wealthy man, whomsoever he may be, for whom I have the greatest contempt, I would fight for him, and you would if you were worth your salt. He should have justice. For every special interest is entitled to justice, but not one is entitled to a vote in Congress, to a voice on the bench, or to representation in any public office. The Constitution guarantees protection to property, and we must make that promise good. But it does not give the right of suffrage to any corporation.

The true friend of property, the true conservative, is he who insists that property shall be the servant and not the master of the commonwealth; who insists that the creature of man's making shall be the servant and not the master of the man who made it. The citizens of the

United States must effectively control the mighty commercial forces which they have them-selves called into being.

There can be no effective control of corporations while their political activity remains. To put an end to it will be neither a short nor an easy task, but it can be done.

We must have complete and effective publicity of corporate affairs, so that the people may know beyond peradventure whether the corporations obey the law and whether their man-agement entitles them to the confidence of the public. It is necessary that laws should be passed to prohibit the use of corporate funds directly or indirectly for political purposes; it is still more necessary that such laws should be thoroughly enforced. Corporate expenditures for political purposes, and especially such expenditures by public service corporations, have supplied one of the principal sources of corruption in our political affairs.

It has become entirely clear that we must have government supervision of the capitalization, not only of public service corporations, including, particularly, railways, but of all corpora-tions doing an interstate business. I do not wish to see the nation forced into the ownership of the railways if it can possibly be avoided, and the only alternative is thoroughgoing and effec-tive regulation, which shall be based on a full knowledge of all the facts, including a physical valuation of property. . . . It is my personal belief that the same kind and degree of control and supervision which should be exercised over public service corporations should be extended also to combinations which control necessaries of life, such as meat, oil, and coal, or which deal in them on an important scale. . . .

I believe that the officers, and, especially, the directors, of corporations should be held per-sonally responsible when any corporation breaks the law.

Combinations in industry are the result of an imperative economic law which cannot be repealed by political legislation. The effort at prohibiting all combination has substantially failed. The way out lies, not in attempting to prevent such combinations, but in completely controlling them in the interest of the public welfare. For that purpose the Federal Bureau of Corporations is an agency of first importance. Its powers, and, therefore, its efficiency, as well as that of the Interstate Commerce Commission, should be largely increased. . . . The Hepburn Act, and the amendment to the Act in the shape in which it finally passed Congress at the last session, represent a long step in advance, and we must go yet further.

The absence of effective state, and, especially, national, restraint upon unfair money getting has tended to create a small class of enormously wealthy and economically powerful men, whose chief object is to hold and increase their power. The prime need is to change the conditions which enable these men to accumulate power which it is not for the general welfare that they should hold or exercise. We grudge no man a fortune which represents his own power and sagacity, when exercised with entire regard to the welfare of his fellows. Again, comrades over there, take the lesson from your own experience. Not only did you not grudge, but you gloried in the promotion of the great generals who gained their promotion by leading the army to victory. So it is with us. We grudge no man a fortune in civil life if it is honorably obtained and well used. It is not even enough that it should have been gained without doing damage to the community. We should permit it to be gained only so long as the gaining represents benefit to the community. This, I know, implies a policy of a far more active governmental interference with social and economic conditions in this country than we have yet had, but I think we have got to face the fact that such an increase in governmental control is now necessary. . . .

The really big fortune, the swollen fortune, by the mere fact of its size acquires qualities which differentiate it in kind as well as in degree from what is possessed by men of relatively small means. Therefore, I believe in a graduated income tax on big fortunes, and in another tax which is far more easily collected and far more effective—a graduated inheritance tax on big fortunes, properly safeguarded against evasion and increasing rapidly in amount with the size of the estate. . . .

Of conservation I shall speak more at length elsewhere. Conservation means development as much as it does protection. I recognize the right and duty of this generation to develop and use the natural resources of our land; but I do not recognize the right to waste them, or to rob, by wasteful use, the generations that come after us. I ask nothing of the nation except that it so behave as each farmer here behaves with reference to his own children. . . . I believe that the natural resources must be used for the benefit of all our people, and not monopolized for the benefit of the few, and here again is another case in which I am accused of taking a revolutionary attitude. . . . Now, with the water power, with the forests, with the mines, we are brought face to face with the fact that there are many people who will go with us in conserving the resources only if they are to be allowed to exploit them for their benefit. That is one of the fundamental reasons why the special interests should be driven out of politics. Of all the questions which can come before this nation, short of the actual preservation of its existence in a great war, there is none which compares in importance with the great central task of leaving this land even a better land for our descendants than it is for us, and training them into a better race to inhabit the land and pass it on. Conservation is a great moral issue, for it involves the patriotic duty of insuring the safety and continuance of the nation. . . in this great work the national government must bear a most important part. . . .

Nothing is more true than that excess of every kind is followed by reaction; a fact which should be pondered by reformer and reactionary alike. We are face to face with new conceptions of the relations of property to human welfare, chiefly because certain advocates of the rights of property as against the rights of men have been pushing their claims too far. The man who wrongly holds that every human right is secondary to his profit must now give way to the advocate of human welfare, who rightly maintains that every man holds his property subject to the general right of the community to regulate its use to whatever degree the public welfare may require it.

But I think we may go still further. The right to regulate the use of wealth in the public interest is universally admitted. Let us admit also the right to regulate the terms and conditions of labor, which is the chief element of wealth, directly in the interest of the common good. The fundamental thing to do for every man is to give him a chance to reach a place in which he will make the greatest possible contribution to the public welfare. Understand what I say there. Give him a chance, not push him up if he will not be pushed. Help any man who stumbles; if he lies down, it is a poor job to try to carry him; but if he is a worthy man, try your best to see that he gets a chance to show the worth that is in him. No man can be a good citizen unless he has a wage more than sufficient to cover the bare cost of living, and hours of labor short enough so that after his day's work is done he will have time and energy to bear his share in the management of the community, to help in carrying the general load. We keep countless men from being good citizens by the conditions of life with which we surround them. We need comprehensive workmen's compensation acts, both state and national laws to regulate child labor and work for women, and, especially, we need in our common schools not merely education in book learning, but also practical training for daily life and work. We need to enforce better sanitary conditions for our workers and to extend the use of safety appliances for our workers in industry and commerce, both within and between the states. Also, friends, in the interest of the workingman himself we need to set our faces like flint against mob violence just as against corporate greed; against violence and injustice and lawlessness by wage workers just as much as against lawless cunning and greed and selfish arrogance of employers. If I could ask but one thing of my fellow countrymen, my request would be that, whenever they go in for reform, they remember the two sides, and that they always exact justice from one side as much as from the other. I have small use for the public servant who can always see and denounce the corruption of the capitalist, but who cannot persuade himself, especially before election, to say a word about lawless mob violence. And I have equally small use for the man, be he a judge on the bench, or editor of a great paper, or wealthy and influential private citizen, who can see clearly enough and denounce the lawlessness of mob violence, but whose eyes are closed so that he is blind when the question is one of corruption in business on a gigantic scale.

Also remember what I said about excess in reformer and reactionary alike. If the reactionary man, who thinks of nothing but the rights of property, could have his way, he would bring about a revolution; and one of my chief fears in connection with progress comes because I do not want to see our people, for lack of proper leadership, compelled to follow men whose intentions are excellent, but whose eyes are a little too wild to make it really safe to trust them. Here in Kansas there is one paper which habitually denounces me as the tool of Wall Street, and at the same time frantically repudiates the statement that I am a Socialist on the ground that that is an unwarranted slander of the Socialists.

National efficiency has many factors. It is a necessary result of the principle of conservation widely applied. In the end it will determine our failure or success as a nation. National efficiency has to do, not only with natural resources and with men, but it is equally concerned with institutions. The state must be made efficient for the work which concerns only the people of the state; and the nation for that which concerns all the people. . . .

I do not ask for over-centralization; but I do ask that we work in a spirit of broad and far-reaching nationalism when we work for what concerns our people as a whole. We are all Americans. Our common interests are as broad as the continent. I speak to you here in Kansas exactly as I would speak in New York or Georgia, for the most vital problems are those which affect us all alike. The national government belongs to the whole American people, and where the whole American people are interested, that interest can be guarded effectively only by the national government. The betterment which we seek must be accomplished, I believe, mainly through the national government.

The American people are right in demanding that New Nationalism, without which we cannot hope to deal with new problems. The New Nationalism puts the national need before sectional or personal advantage. It is impatient of the utter confusion that results from local legislatures attempting to treat national issues as local issues. It is still more impatient of the impotence which springs from over-division of governmental powers, the impotence which makes it possible for local selfishness or for legal cunning, hired by wealthy special interests, to bring national activities to a deadlock. This New Nationalism regards the executive power as the steward of the public welfare. It demands of the judiciary that it shall be interested primarily in human welfare rather than in property, just as it demands that the representative body shall represent all the people rather than any one class or section of the people. I believe in shaping the ends of government to protect property as well as human welfare. . . . I am far from underestimating the importance of dividends; but I rank dividends below human character. Again, I do not have any sympathy with the reformer who says he does not care for dividends. Of course, economic welfare is necessary, for a man must pull his own weight and be able to support his family. I know well that the reformers must not bring upon the people economic ruin, or the reforms themselves will go down in the ruin. But we must be ready to face temporary disaster, whether or not brought on by those who will war against us to the knife. Those who oppose all reform will do well to remember that ruin in its worst form is inevitable if our national life brings us nothing better than swollen fortunes for the few and the triumph in both politics and business of a sordid and selfish materialism.

If our political institutions were perfect, they would absolutely prevent the political domination of money in any part of our affairs. . . .

One of the fundamental necessities in a representative government such as ours is to make certain that the men to whom the people delegate their power shall serve the people by whom they are elected, and not the special interests. . . . The object of government is the welfare of the people. The material progress and prosperity of a nation are desirable chiefly so far as they lead to the moral and material welfare of all good citizens. . . . We must have—I believe we have already—a genuine and permanent moral awakening, without which no wisdom of legislation or administration really means anything; and, on the other hand, we must try to secure the social and economic legislation without which any improvement due to purely moral agitation is necessarily evanescent. . . .

No matter how honest and decent we are in our private lives, if we do not have the right kind of law and the right kind of administration of the law, we cannot go forward as a nation. That is imperative; but it must be an addition to, and not a substitution for, the qualities that make us good citizens. In the last analysis, the most important elements in any man's career must be the sum of those qualities which, in the aggregate, we speak of as character. If he has not got it, then no law that the wit of man can devise, no administration of the law by the boldest and strongest executive, will avail to help him. We must have the right kind of character—character that makes a man, first of all, a good man in the home, a good father, a good husband—that makes a man a good neighbor. You must have that, and, then, in addition, you must have the kind of law and the kind of administration of the law which will give to those qualities in the private citizen the best possible chance for development. The prime problem of our nation is to get the right type of good citizenship, and, to get it, we must have progress, and our public men must be genuinely progressive.

Document Twenty-Six

Jane Addams Analyzes the Motivations of the Settlement House Movement

Context: *The settlement house movement attempted to connect members of the upper and middle classes with the urban poor. By 1910, more than 400 settlement homes existed in the United States. The majority of residents were much like Jane Addams: idealistic, educated women seeking to make a difference. In 1899, Addams and Ellen Gates Starr moved to Chicago and founded Hull House, which quickly became the best known settlement house. Hull House provided a wide array of services to the many immigrants in the surrounding neighborhoods. Addams's energy, idealism, and accomplishments made her one of the most admired figures during the Progressive Era.*

Questions to Consider: *According to Addams, what three impulses motivated the settlement house movement and what social groups would benefit from the movement? In what ways would the settlement house movement revitalize American democracy? What social problems did the settlements hope to address? Compare and contrast Addams's understanding of the settlement house movement with Roosevelt's New Nationalism. What aspirations did TR and Addams share? In what ways did their approach to reform differ?*

Jane Addams, Subjective Necessity for Social Settlements (From *Twenty Years at Hull-House with Autobiographical Notes. (c.1910): 113–127*

This paper is an attempt to analyze the motives which underlie a movement based, not only upon conviction, but upon genuine emotion, wherever educated young people are seeking an outlet for that sentiment for universal brotherhood, which the best spirit of our times is forcing from an emotion into a motive. These young people accomplish little toward the solution of this social problem, and bear the brunt of being cultivated into unnourished, oversensitive lives. They have been shut off from the common labor by which they live which is a great source of moral and physical health. They feel a fatal want of harmony between their theory and their lives, a lack of coördination between thought and action. I think it is hard for us to realize how seriously many of them are taking to the notion of human brotherhood, how eagerly they long to give tangible expression to the democratic ideal. These young men and women, longing to socialize their democracy, are animated by certain hopes which may be thus loosely formulated; that if in a democratic country nothing can be permanently achieved save through the masses of the people, it will be impossible to establish a higher political life than the people themselves crave; that it is difficult to see how the notion of a higher civic life can be fostered save through common intercourse; that the blessings which we associate with a life of refinement and cultivation can be made universal and must be made universal if they are to be permanent; that the good we secure for ourselves is precarious and uncertain, is floating in mid-air, until it is secured for all of us and incorporated into our common life. It is easier to state these hopes than to formulate the line of motives, which I believe to constitute the trend of the subjective pressure toward the Settlement. . . .

You may remember the forlorn feeling which occasionally seizes you when you arrive early in the morning a stranger in a great city: the stream of laboring people goes past you as you gaze through the plate-glass window of your hotel; you see hard working men lifting great burdens; you hear the driving and jostling of huge carts and your heart sinks with a sudden sense of futility. The door opens behind you and you turn to the man who brings you in your breakfast with a quick sense of human fellowship. You find yourself praying that you may never lose your hold on it all. A more poetic prayer would be that the great mother breasts of our common humanity, with its labor and suffering and its homely comforts, may never be withheld from you. You turn helplessly to the waiter and feel that it would be almost grotesque to claim from him the sympathy you crave because civilization has placed you apart, but you resent your position with a sudden sense of snobbery. . . .

. . . In our attempt then to give a girl pleasure and freedom from care we succeed, for the most part, in making her pitifully miserable. She finds "life" so different from what she expected it to be. She is besotted with innocent little ambitions, and does not understand this apparent waste of herself, this elaborate preparation, if no work is provided for her. There is a heritage of noble obligation which young people accept and long to perpetuate. The desire for action, the wish to right wrong and alleviate suffering haunts them daily. Society smiles at it indulgently instead of making it of value to itself. The wrong to them begins even farther back, when we restrain the first childish desires for "doing good", and tell them that they must wait until they are older and better fitted. We intimate that social obligation begins at a fixed date, forgetting that it begins at birth itself. We treat them as children who, with strong-growing limbs, are allowed to use their legs but not their arms, or whose legs are daily carefully exercised that after a while their arms may be put to high use. We do this in spite of the protest of the best educators, Locke and Pestalozzi. We are fortunate in the meantime if their unused members do not weaken and disappear. They do sometimes. There are a few girls who, by the time they are "educated," forget their old childish desires to help the world and to play with poor little girls "who haven't playthings". Parents are often inconsistent: they deliberately expose their daughters to knowledge of the distress in the world; they send them to hear missionary addresses on famines in India and China; they accompany them to lectures on the suffering in Siberia; they agitate together over the forgotten region of East London. In addition to this, from babyhood the altruistic tendencies of these daughters are persistently cultivated. They are taught to be self-forgetting and self-sacrificing, to consider the good of the whole before the good of the ego. But when all this information and culture show results, when the daughter comes back from college and begins to recognize her social claim to the "submerged tenth", and to evince a disposition to fulfill it, the family claim is strenuously asserted; she is told that she is unjustified, ill-advised in her efforts. If she persists, the family too often are injured and unhappy unless the efforts are called missionary and the religious zeal of the family carry them over their sense of abuse. When this zeal does not exist, the result is perplexing. It is a curious violation of what we would fain believe a fundamental law—that the final return of the deed is upon the head of the doer. The deed is that of exclusiveness and caution, but the return, instead of falling upon the head of the exclusive and cautious, falls upon a young head full of generous and unselfish plans. The girl loses something vital out of her life to which she is entitled. She is restricted and unhappy; her elders meanwhile, are unconscious of the situation and we have all the elements of a tragedy.

We have in America a fast-growing number of cultivated young people who have no recognized outlet for their active faculties. They hear constantly of the great social maladjustment, but no way is provided for them to change it, and their uselessness hangs about them heavily. . . . These young people have had advantages of college, of European travel, and of economic study, but they are sustaining this shock of inaction. They have pet phrases, and they tell you that the things that make us all alike are stronger than the things that make us different. They say that all men are united by needs and sympathies far more permanent and radical than anything that temporarily divides them and sets them in opposition to each other. . . . They tell their elders with all the bitterness of youth that if they expect success from them in business or politics or in whatever lines their ambition for them has run, they must let them consult all of humanity; that they must let them find out what the people want and how they want it. It is only the stronger young people, however, who formulate this. Many of them dissipate their energies in so-called enjoyment. Others not content with that, go on studying and go back to college for their second degrees; not that they are especially fond of study, but because they want something definite to do, and their powers have been trained in the direction of mental accumulation. Many are buried beneath this mental accumulation with lowered vitality and discontent. Walter Besant says they have had the vision that Peter had when he saw the great sheet let down from heaven, wherein was neither clean nor unclean. He calls it the sense of humanity. It is not philanthropy nor benevolence, but a thing fuller and wider than either of these.

This young life, so sincere in its emotion and good phrases and yet so undirected, seems to me as pitiful as the other great mass of destitute lives. One is supplementary to the other, and some method of communication can surely be devised. Mr. Barnett, who urged the first

Settlement,—Toynbee Hall, in East London,—recognized this need of outlet for the young men of Oxford and Cambridge, and hoped that the Settlement would supply the communication. It is easy to see why the Settlement movement originated in England, where the years of education are more constrained and definite than they are here, where class distinctions are more rigid. The necessity of it was greater there, but we are fast feeling the pressure of the need and meeting the necessity for Settlements in America. Our young people feel nervously the need of putting theory into action, and respond quickly to the Settlement form of activity.

Other motives which I believe make toward the Settlement are the result of a certain renaissance going forward in Christianity. The impulse to share the lives of the poor, the desire to make social service, irrespective of propaganda, express the spirit of Christ, is as old as Christianity itself. . . . Jesus had no set of truths labeled Religious. On the contrary, his doctrine was that all truth is one, that the appropriation of it is freedom. His teaching had no dogma to mark it off from truth and action in general. He himself called it a revelation—a life. . . . The Christians looked for the continuous revelation, but believed what Jesus said, that this revelation, to be retained and made manifest, must be put into terms of action; that action is the only medium man has for receiving and appropriating truth; that the doctrine must be known through the will.

That Christianity has to be revealed and embodied in the line of social progress is a corollary to the simple proposition, that man's action is found in his social relationships in the way in which he connects with his fellows; that his motives for action are the zeal and affection with which he regards his fellows. By this simple process was created a deep enthusiasm for humanity; which regarded man as at once the organ and the object of revelation; and by this process came about the wonderful fellowship, the true democracy of the early Church, that so captivates the imagination. . . . The spectacle of the Christians loving all men was the most astounding Rome had ever seen. They were eager to sacrifice themselves for the weak, for children, and for the aged; they identified themselves with slaves and did not avoid the plague; they longed to share the common lot that they might receive the constant revelation. It was a new treasure which the early Christians added to the sum of all treasures, a joy hitherto unknown in the world—the joy of finding the Christ which lieth in each man, but which no man can unfold save in fellowship. . . .

I believe that there is a distinct turning among many young men and women toward this simple acceptance of Christ's message. They resent the assumption that Christianity is a set of ideas which belong to the religious consciousness, whatever that may be. They insist that it cannot be proclaimed and instituted apart from the social life of the community and that it must seek a simple and natural expression in the social organism itself. The Settlement movement is only one manifestation of that wider humanitarian movement which throughout Christendom, but pre-eminently in England, is endeavoring to embody itself, not in a sect, but in society itself.

I believe that this turning, this renaissance of the early Christian humanitarianism, is going on in America, in Chicago, if you please, without leaders who write or philosophize, without much speaking, but with a bent to express in social service and in terms of action the spirit of Christ. Certain it is that spiritual force is found in the Settlement movement, and it is also true that this force must be evoked and must be called into play before the success of any Settlement is assured. There must be the overmastering belief that all that is noblest in life is common to men as men, in order to accentuate the likenesses and ignore the differences which are found among the people whom the Settlement constantly brings into juxtaposition. It may be true, as the Positivists insist, that the very religious fervor of man can be turned into love for his race, and his desire for a future life into content to live in the echo of his deeds; Paul's formula of seeking for the Christ which lieth in each man and founding our likenesses on him, seems a simpler formula to many of us.

In a thousand voices singing the Hallelujah Chorus in Handel's "Messiah," it is possible to distinguish the leading voices, but the differences of training and cultivation between them and the voices in the chorus, are lost in the unity of purpose and in the fact that they are all human voices lifted by a high motive. This is a weak illustration of what a Settlement attempts to do. It aims, in a measure, to develop whatever of social life its neighborhood may afford, to focus and give form to that life, to bring to bear upon it the results of cultivation and training; but it receives in exchange for the music of isolated voices the volume and strength of the chorus. It is quite impossible for me to say in what proportion or degree the subjective necessity which led to the opening of Hull-House combined the three trends: first, the desire to interpret democracy in social terms; secondly, the impulse beating at the very source of our lives, urging us to aid in the race progress; and, thirdly, the Christian movement toward humanitarianism. . . .

The Settlement then, is an experimental effort to aid in the solution of the social and industrial problems which are engendered by the modern conditions of life in a great city. It insists that these problems are not confined to any one portion of a city. It is an attempt to relieve, at the same time, the overaccumulation at one end of society and the destitution at the other; but it assumes that this overaccumulation and destitution is most sorely felt in the things that pertain to social and educational privileges.

. . . The only thing to be dreaded in the Settlement is that it lose its flexibility, its power of quick adaptation, its readiness to change its methods as its environment may demand. It must be open to conviction and must have a deep and abiding sense of tolerance. It must be hospitable and ready for experiment. It should demand from its residents a scientific patience in the accumulation of facts and the steady holding of their sympathies as one of the best instruments for that accumulation. It must be grounded in a philosophy whose foundation is on the solidarity of the human race, a philosophy which will not waver when the race happens to be represented by a drunken woman or an idiot boy. Its residents must be emptied of all conceit of opinion and all self-assertion, and ready to arouse and interpret the public opinion of their neighborhood. They must be content to live quietly side by side with their neighbors, until they grow into a sense of relationship and mutual interests. Their neighbors are held apart by differences of race and language which the residents can more easily overcome. They are bound to see the needs of their neighborhood as a whole, to furnish data for legislation, and to use their influence to secure it. In short, residents are pledged to devote themselves to the duties of good citizenship and to the arousing of the social energies which too largely lie dormant in every neighborhood given over to industrialism. They are bound to regard the entire life of their city as organic, to make an effort to unify it, and to protest against its over-differentiation.

It is always easy to make all philosophy point one particular moral and all history adorn one particular tale; but I may be forgiven the reminder that the best speculative philosophy sets forth the solidarity of the human race; that the highest moralists have taught that without the advance and improvement of the whole, no man can hope for any lasting improvement in his own moral or material individual condition; and that the subjective necessity for Social Settlements is therefore identical with that necessity, which urges us on toward social and individual salvation.

Document Twenty-Seven

Jacob Riis Exposes Poverty in New York City

Context: *Jacob Riis was a Danish-born photographer and journalist. He was part of a journalistic movement called "muckraking," which sought to instigate political change by exposing corporate abuses, political corruption, and social evils. Effectively combining the written word with photographs to publicize poverty in the New York City, Riis became a particularly influential reformer. "The Problem of Children" is a chapter of* How the Other Half Lives *(1890), which became a landmark in the social reform literature.*

Questions to Consider: *How did Riis portray immigrant culture? Who did Riis blame for the condition of immigrant children? Why do you think Riis focused so heavily on the plight of children to arouse reform? Do you see any connections between Riis and abolitionist reformers of the previous generation? How did Riis's rhetoric strengthen and weaken his advocacy for immigrants?*

"The Problem of the Children" (1890)

The problem of the children becomes, in these swarms, to the last degree perplexing. Their very number make one stand aghast. I have already given instances of the packing of the child population in East Side tenements. They might be continued indefinitely until the array would be enough to startle any community. For, be it remembered, these children with the training they receive—or do not receive—with the instincts they inherit and absorb in their growing up, are to be our future rulers, if our theory of government is worth anything. More than a working majority of our voters now register from the tenements. I counted the other day the little ones, up to ten years or so, in a Bayard Street tenement . . . I tried to count the children that swarmed there, but could not. Sometimes I have doubted that anybody knows just how many there are about. Bodies of drowned children turn up in the rivers right along sin summer whom no one seems to know anything about. When last spring some workmen, while moving a pile of lumber on a North River pier, found under the last plank the body of a little lad crushed to death, no one had missed a boy, though his parents afterward turned up. The truant officer assuredly does not know, though he spends his life trying to find out, somewhat illogically, perhaps, since the department that employs him admits that thousands of poor children are crowded out of the schools year by year for want of room. . . . .

The old question, what to do with the boy, assumes a new and serious phase in the tenements. Under the best conditions found there, it is not easily answered. In nine cases out of ten he would make an excellent mechanic, if trained early to work at a trade, for he is neither dull nor slow, but the short-sighted despotism of the trades unions has practically closed that avenue to him. Trade-schools, however excellent, cannot supply the opportunity thus denied him, and at the outset the boy stands condemned by his own to low and ill-paid drudgery, held down by the hand that of all should labor to raise him. Home, the greatest factor of all in the training of the young, means nothing to him but a pigeon-hole in a coop along with so many other human animals. Its influence is scarcely of the elevating kind, if it have any. The very games at which he takes a hand in the street become polluting in its atmosphere. With no steady hand to guide him, the boy takes naturally to idle ways. Caught in the street by the truant officer, or by the agents of the Children's Societies, peddling, perhaps, or begging, to help out the family resources; he runs the risk of being sent to a reformatory, where contact with vicious boys older than himself soon develop the latent possibilities for evil that lie hidden in him. The city has no Truant Home in which to keep him, and all efforts of the children's friends to enforce school attendance are paralyzed by this want. The risk of the reformatory is too great. What is done in the end is to let him take chances—with the chances all against him. The result is the rough young savage, familiar from the street.

. . . A little fellow who seemed clad in but a single rag was among the flotsam and jetsam stranded at Police Headquarters one day last summer. No one knew where he came from or where he belonged. . . . The examination went on after this fashion:

"Where do you go to church, my boy?"

"We don't have no clothes to go to church." And indeed his appearance, as he was, in the door of any New York church would have caused a sensation.

"Well, where do you go to school, then?"

"I don't go to school," with a snort of contempt.

"Where do you buy your bread?"

"We don't buy no bread; we buy beer," said the boy, and it was eventually the saloon that led the police as a landmark to his "home." It was worthy of the boy. As he had said, his only bed was a heap of dirty straw on the floor, his daily diet a crust in the morning, nothing else.

Into the rooms of the Children's Aid Society were led two little girls whose father had "busted up the house "and put them on the street after their mother died. Another, who was turned out by her stepmother" because she had five of her own and could not afford to keep her," could not remember ever having been in church or Sunday-school, and only knew the name of Jesus through hearing people swear by it. She had no idea what they meant. These were specimens of the overflow from the tenements of our home-heathen that are growing up in New York's streets to-day, while tender-hearted men and women are busying themselves with the socks and the hereafter of well-fed little Hottentots thousands of miles away. According to Canon Taylor, of York, one hundred and nine missionaries in the four fields of Persia, Palestine, Arabia, and Egypt spent one year and sixty thousand dollars in converting one little heathen girl. If there is nothing the matter with those missionaries, they might come to New York with a good deal better prospect of success. . . .

Nothing is now better understood than that the rescue of the children is the key to the problem of city poverty, as presented for our solution today; that character may be formed where to reform it would be a hopeless task. The concurrent testimony of all who have to undertake it at a later stage: that the young are naturally neither vicious nor hardened, simply weak and undeveloped, except by the bad influences of the street, makes this duty all the more urgent as well as hopeful. Helping hands are held out on every side. To private charity the municipality leaves the entire care of its proletariat of tender years, lulling its conscience to sleep with liberal appropriations of money to foot the bills. Indeed, it is held by those whose opinions are entitled to weight that it is far too liberal a paymaster for its own best interests and those of its wards. It deals with the evil in the seed to a limited extent in gathering in the outcast babies from the streets. To the ripe fruit the gates of its prisons, its reformatories, and its workhouses are opened wide the year round. What the showing would be at this end of the line were it not for the barriers wise charity has thrown across the broad highway to ruin—is building day by day—may be measured by such results as those quoted above in the span of a single life.

Document Twenty-Eight

Anzia Yezierska Describes Conflict between Immigrants and Reformers

Context: *During the Progressive Era, tens of millions of emigrants left Eastern and Southern Europe to live in the United States. Anzia Yezierska's family emigrated from Poland when she was a young child. She worked to help support her large family by selling newspapers, which was a common experience for many immigrant children. After winning a scholarship to the American Academy in 1907, she became a successful writer, often focusing on the experiences of immigrant women. This story is drawn from her book* Hungry Hearts, *which was published in 1920.*

Questions to Consider: *In what ways is the title of the story ("The Free Vacation House") ironic? What does the vacation house come to symbolize? What does this story reveal about the motives of Progressive reformers? Is it fair to characterize all reformers in this light? To what extent do you think Yezierska would have agreed with Andrew Carnegie's conception of charity? How might have Jane Addams and Jacob Riis reacted to this story?*

"The Free Vacation House" (1920)

How came it that I went to the free vacation house was like this:

One day the visiting teacher from the school comes to find out for why don't I get the children ready for school in time; for why are they so often late.

I let out on her my whole bitter heart. I told her my head was on wheels from worrying. When I get up in the morning, I don't know on what to turn first: should I nurse the baby, or make Sam's breakfast, or attend on the older children. I only got two hands.

"My dear woman," she says, "you are about to have a nervous breakdown. You need to get away to the country for a rest and vacation."

"Gott im Himmel!" says I. "Don't I know I need a rest? But how? On what money can I go to the country?"

"I know of a nice country place for mothers and children that will not cost you anything. It is free."

"Free! I never heard from it."

"Some kind people have made arrangements so no one need pay," she explains.

Later, in a few days, I just finished up with Masha and Mendel and Frieda and Sonya to send them to school, and I was getting Aby ready for kindergarten, when I hear a knock on the door, and a lady comes in. She had a white starched dress like a nurse and carried a black satchel in her hand.

"I am from the Social Betterment Society," she tells me. "You want to go to the country?"

Before I could say something, she goes over to the baby and pulls out the rubber nipple from her mouth, and to me she says, "You must not get the child used to sucking this; it is very unsanitary."

"Gott im Himmel!" I beg the lady. "Please don't begin with that child, or she'll holler my head off. She must have the nipple. I'm too nervous to hear her scream like that."

When I put the nipple back again in the baby's mouth, the lady takes herself a seat, and then takes out a big black book from her satchel. Then she begins to question me. What is my first name? How old I am? From where come I? How long I'm already in this country? Do I keep any boarders? What is my husband's first name? How old he is? How long he is in this country? By what trade he works? How much wages he gets for a week? How much money do I spend out for rent? How old are the children, and everything about them.

"My goodness!" I cry out. "For why is it necessary all this to know? For why must I tell you all my business? What difference does it make already if I keep boarders, or I don't keep boarders? If Masha had the whooping-cough or Sonya had the measles? Or whether I spend out for my rent ten dollars or twenty? Or whether I come from Schnipishock or Kovner Gubernie?"

"We must make a record of all the applicants, and investigate each case," she tells me. "There are so many who apply to the charities, we can help only those who are the most worthy."

"Charities!" I scream out. "Ain't the charities those who help the beggars out? I ain't no beggar. I'm not asking for no charity. My husband, he works."

"Miss Holcomb, the visiting teacher, said that you wanted to go to the country, and I had to make out this report before investigating your case."

"Oh! Oh!" I choke and bit my lips. "Is the free country from which Miss Holcomb told me, is it from the charities? She was telling me some kind people made arrangements for any mother what needs to go there."

158   **History of the American Peoples**

"If your application is approved, you will be notified," she says to me, and out she goes.

When she is gone I think to myself, I'd better knock out from my head this idea about the country. For so long I lived, I didn't know nothing about the charities. For why should I come down among the beggars now?

Then I looked around me in the kitchen. On one side was the big wash-tub with clothes, waiting for me to wash. On the table was a pile of breakfast dishes yet. In the sink was the potatoes, waiting to be peeled. The baby was beginning to cry for the bottle. Aby was hollering and pulling me to take him to kindergarten. I felt if I didn't get away from here for a little while, I would land in a crazy house, or from the window jump down. Which was worser, to land in a crazy house, jump from the window down, or go to the country from the charities?

In about two weeks later around comes the same lady with the satchel again in my house.

"You can go to the country to-morrow," she tells me. "And you must come to the charity building to-morrow at nine o'clock sharp. Here is a card with the address. Don't lose it, because you must hand it to the lady in the office."

I look on the card, and there I see my name wrote; and by it, in big printed letters, that word "CHARITY."

"Must I go to the charity office?" I ask, feeling my heart to sink. "For why must I come there?"

"It is the rule that everybody comes to the office first, and from there they are taken to the country."

I shivered to think how I would feel, suppose somebody from my friends should see me walking to the charity office with my children. They wouldn't know that it is only for the country I go there. They might think I go to beg. Have I come down so low as to be seen by the charities? But what's the use? Should I knock my head on the walls? I had to go.

When I come to the office, I already found a crowd of women and children sitting on long benches and waiting. I took myself a seat with them, and we were sitting and sitting and looking on one another, sideways and crosswise, and with lowered eyes, like guilty criminals. Each one felt like hiding herself from all the rest. Each one felt black with shame in the face.

We may have been sitting and waiting for an hour or more. But every second was seeming years to me. The children began to get restless. Mendel wanted water. The baby on my arms was falling asleep. Aby was crying for something to eat.

"For why are we sittin' here like fat cats?" says the woman next to me. "Ain't we going to the country today yet?"

At last a lady comes to the desk and begins calling us our names, one by one. I nearly dropped to the floor when over she begins to ask: Do you keep boarders? How much do you spend out for rent? How much wages does your man get for a week?

Didn't the nurse tell them all about us already? It was bitter enough to have to tell the nurse everything, but in my own house nobody was hearing my troubles, only the nurse. But in the office there was so many strangers all around me. For why should everybody have to know my business? At every question I wanted to holler out: "Stop! Stop! I don't want no vacations! I'll better run home with my children." At every question I felt like she was stabbing a knife into my heart. And she kept on stabbing me more and more, but I could not help it, and they were all looking at me. I couldn't move from her. I had to answer everything.

When she got through with me, my face was red like fire. I was burning with hurts and wounds. I felt like everything was bleeding in me.

When all the names was already called, a man doctor with a nurse comes in, and tells us to form a line, to be examined. I wish I could ease out my heart a little, and tell in words how that doctor looked on us, just because we were poor and had no money to pay. He only used the ends, from his finger-tips to examine us with. From the way he was afraid to touch us or come near us, he made us feel like we had some catching sickness that he was trying not to get on him.

The doctor got finished with us in about five minutes, so quick he worked. Then we was told to walk after the nurse, who was leading the way for us through the street to the car. Everybody what passed us in the street turned around to look on us. I kept down my eyes and held down my head and I felt like sinking into the sidewalk. All the time I was trembling for fear somebody what knows me might yet pass and see me. For why did they make us walk through the street, after the nurse, like stupid cows? Weren't all of us smart enough to find our way without the nurse? Why should the whole world have to see that we are from the charities?

When we got into the train, I opened my eyes, and lifted up my head, and straightened out my chest, and again began to breathe. It was a beautiful, sunshiny day. I knocked open the window from the train, and the fresh-smelling country air rushed upon my face and made me feel so fine! I looked out from the window and instead of seeing the iron fire-escapes with garbage-cans and bedclothes, that I always seen when from my flat I looked—instead of seeing only walls and wash-lines between walls, I saw the blue sky, and green grass, and trees and flowers.

Ah, how grand I felt, just on the sky to look! Ah, how grand I felt just to see the green grass—and the free space—and no houses!

"Get away from me, my troubles!" I said. "Leave me rest a minute. Leave me breathe and straighten out my bones. Forget the unpaid butcher's bill. Forget the rent. Forget the wash-tub and the cook-stove and the pots and pans. Forget the charities!"

"Tickets, please," calls the train conductor.

I felt knocked out from heaven all at once. I had to point to the nurse who held our tickets, and I was feeling the conductor looking on me as if to say, "Oh, you are only from the charities."

By the time we came to the vacation house I already forgot all about my knock-down. I was again filled with the beauty of the country. I never in all my life yet seen such a swell house like that vacation house. Like the grandest palace it looked. All round the front, flowers from all colors was smelling out the sweetest perfume. Here and there was shady trees with comfortable chairs under them to sit down on.

When I only came inside, my mouth opened wide and my breathing stopped still from wonder. I never yet seen such an order and such a cleanliness. From all the corners from the room, the cleanliness was shining like a looking-glass. The floor was so white scrubbed you could eat on it. You couldn't find a speck of dust on nothing, if you was looking for it with eyeglasses on.

I was beginning to feel happy and glad that I come, when, Gott im Himmel! again a lady begins to ask us out the same questions what the nurse already asked me in my home and what was asked over again in the charity office. How much wages my husband makes out for a week? How much money I spend out for rent? Do I keep boarders?

We were hungry enough to faint. So worn out was I from excitement, and from the long ride, that my knees were bending under me ready to break from tiredness. The children were pulling me to pieces, nagging me for a drink, for something to eat and such like. But still we had to stand out the whole list of questionings. When she already got through asking us out everything, she gave to each of us a tag with our name written on it. She told us to tie the tag on our hand. Then like tagged horses at a horse sale in the street, they marched us into the dining-room.

There was rows of long tables, covered with the pure-white oil-cloth. A vase with bought flowers was standing on the middle from each table. Each person got a clean napkin for himself. Laid out by the side from each person's plate was a silver knife and fork and spoon and teaspoon. When we only sat ourselves down, girls with white starched aprons was passing around the eatings.

I soon forgot again all my troubles. For the first time in ten years I sat down to a meal what I did not have to cook or worry about. For the first time in ten years I sat down to the table like a somebody. Ah, how grand it feels, to have handed you over the eatings and everything you need. Just as I was beginning to like it and let myself feel good, in comes a fat lady all in white, with a teacher's look on her face. I could tell already, right away by the way she looked on us, that she was the boss from this place.

"I want to read you the rules from this house, before you leave this room," says she to us.

Then she began like this: We dassen't stand on the front grass where the flowers are. We dassen't stay on the front porch. We dassen't sit on the chairs under the shady trees. We must stay always in back and sit on those long wooden benches there. We dassen't come in the front sitting-room or walk on the front steps what have carpet on it—we must walk on the back iron steps. Everything on the front from the house must be kept perfect for the show for visitors. We dassen't lay down on the beds in the daytime, the beds must always be made up perfect for the show for visitors.

"Gott im Himmel!" thinks I to myself; "ain't there going to be no end to the things we dassen't do in this place?"

But still she went on. The children over two years dassen't stay around by the mothers. They must stay by the nurse in the play-room. By the meal-times, they can see their mothers. The children dassen't run around the house or tear up flowers or do anything. They dassen't holler or play rough in the play-room. They must always behave and obey the nurse.

We must always listen to the bells. Bell one was for getting up. Bell two, for getting babies' bottles. Bell three, for coming to breakfast. Bell four, for bathing the babies. If we come later, after the ring from the bell, then we'll not get what we need. If the bottle bell rings and we don't come right away for the bottle, then the baby don't get no bottle. If the breakfast bell rings, and we don't come right away down to the breakfast, then there won't be no breakfast for us.

When she got through with reading the rules, I was wondering which side of the house I was to walk on. At every step was some rule what said don't more here, and don't go there, don't stand there, and don't sit there. If I tried to remember the endless rules, it would only make me dizzy in the head. I was thinking for why, with so many rules, didn't they also have already another rule, about how much air in our lungs to breathe.

On every few days there came to the house swell ladies in automobiles. It was for them that the front from the house had to be always perfect. For them was all the beautiful smelling flowers. For them the front porch, the front sitting-room, and the easy stairs with the carpet on it.

Always when the rich ladies came the fat lady, what was the boss from the vacation house, showed off to them the front. Then she took them over to the back to look on us, where we was sitting together, on long wooden benches, like prisoners. I was always feeling cheap like dirt, and mad that I had to be there, when they smiled down on us.

"How nice for these poor creatures to have a restful place like this," I heard one lady say.

The next day I already felt like going back. The children what had to stay by the nurse in the play-room didn't like it neither.

"Mamma," says Mendel to me, "I wisht I was home and out in the street. They don't let us do nothing here. It's worser than school."

"Ain't it a play-room?" asks I. "Don't they let you play?"

"Gee wiss! play-room, they call it! The nurse hollers on us all the time. She don't let us do nothing."

The reason why I stayed out the whole two weeks is this: I think to myself, so much shame in the face I suffered to come here, let me at least make the best from it already. Let me at least save up for two weeks what I got to spend out for grocery and butcher for my back bills to pay out. And then also think I to myself, if I go back on Monday, I got to do the big washing; on Tuesday waits for me the ironing; on Wednesday, the scrubbing and cleaning, and so goes it on. How bad it is already in this place, it's a change from the very sameness of what I'm having day in and day out at home. And so I stayed out this vacation to the bitter end.

But at last the day for going out from this prison came. On the way riding back, I kept thinking to myself: "This is such a beautiful vacation house. For why do they make it so hard for us? When a mother needs a vacation, why must they tear the insides out from her first, by making her come down to the charity office? Why drag us from the charity office through the streets? And when we live through the shame of the charities and when we come already to the vacation house, for why do they boss the life out of us with so many rules and bells? For why don't they let us lay down our heads on the bed when we are tired? For why must we always stick in the back, like dogs what have got to be chained in one spot? If they would let us walk around free, would we bite off something from the front part of the house?

"If the best part of the house what is comfortable is made up for show for visitors, why ain't they keeping the whole business for a show for visitors? For why do they have to fool in worn-out mothers, to make them think they'll give them a rest? Do they need the worn-out mothers as part of the show? I guess that is it, already."

When I got back in my home, so happy and thankful I was I could cry from thankfulness. How good it was feeling for me to be able to move around my own house, like I pleased. I was always kicking that my rooms was small and narrow, but now my small rooms seemed to grow so big like the park. I looked out from my window on the fire-escapes, full with bedding and garbage-cans, and on the wash-lines full with the clothes. All these ugly things was grand in my eyes. Even the high brick walls all around made me feel like a bird that just jumped out of a cage. And I cried out, "Gott sei dank! Gott sei dank!"

Name: _____ Date: _____

Document Analysis Worksheet

  1. Date/Author of Document/Author's Position: Intended Audience:

  2. Why was this document written? List three points the author made that you find important.

  3. List two things the document tells you about life in the United States at the time it was written.

  4. Write a question to the author that the document left unanswered.

Comparative Analysis Worksheet

Choose two documents from this week's readings in which the document authors present different takes on a particular issue.

   1. Identify two or three key points on which the authors agree and/or disagree.

_____

_____

_____

_____

_____

_____

_____

   2. Develop your analysis of these two documents further by answering one or two questions listed in the "Questions to Consider" section for each document.

_____

_____

_____

_____

_____

_____

_____

_____

_____

_____

_____

Document Twenty-Nine

Booker T. Washington Advocates Economic Advancement

Context: *Facing mounting violence and increasingly discriminatory laws, African Americans in the Progressive Era had few viable strategies for economic and political advancement. Booker T. Washington, a former slave and well-known educator, proposed a strategy focusing on economic success. Washington outlined his views before a large audience at the Atlanta Exposition (1895), a large fair that promoted the business prospects of the New South. Washington's speech made him the most influential African American since Frederick Douglass. Washington met frequently with powerful politicians and industrialists, and even dined with TR at the White House in 1901.*

Questions to Consider: *What sort of training and education for African Americans did Washington propose? What did Washington mean when he said, "cast down your bucket where you are"? Did Washington's speech echo any elements of free labor ideology? Why do you think that whites tended to react favorably to Washington's remarks? To what extent did Washington accept segregation as a fact of life? Would Frederick Douglass have agreed with Washington's strategies?*

Booker T. Washington, "The Atlanta Exposition Speech," (1895)

Mr. President and Gentlemen of the Board of Directors and Citizens:

One-third of the population of the South is of the Negro race. No enterprise seeking the material, civil, or moral welfare of this section can disregard this element of our population and reach the highest success. I but convey to you, Mr. President and Directors, the sentiment of the masses of my race when I say that in no way have the value and manhood of the American Negro been more fittingly and generously recognized than by the managers of this magnificent Exposition at every stage of its progress. It is a recognition that will do more to cement the friendship of the two races than any occurrence since the dawn of our freedom.

Not only this, but the opportunity here afforded will awaken among us a new era of industrial progress. Ignorant and inexperienced, it is not strange that in the first years of our new life we began at the top instead of at the bottom; that a seat in Congress or the state legislature was more sought than real estate or industrial skill; that the political convention of stump speaking had more attraction than starting a dairy farm or truck garden.

A ship lost at sea for many days suddenly sighted a friendly vessel. From the mast of the unfortunate vessel was seen a signal, "Water, water; we die of thirst!" The answer from the friendly vessel at once came back, "Cast down your bucket where you are." A second time the signal, "Water, water; send us water!" ran up from the distressed vessel, and was answered, "Cast down your bucket where you are." And a third and fourth signal for water was answered, "Cast down your bucket where you are." The captain of the distressed vessel, at last heeding the injunction, cast down his bucket, and it came up full of fresh, sparkling water from the mouth of the Amazon River. To those of my race who depend on bettering their condition in a foreign land or who underestimate the importance of cultivating friendly relations with the Southern white man, who is their next-door neighbor, I would say: "Cast down your bucket where you are"—cast it down in making friends in every manly way of the people of all races by whom we are surrounded.

Cast it down in agriculture, mechanics, in commerce, in domestic service, and in the professions. And in this connection it is well to bear in mind that whatever other sins the South may be called to bear, when it comes to business, pure and simple, it is in the South that the Negro is given a man's chance in the commercial world, and in nothing is this Exposition more eloquent than in emphasizing this chance. Our greatest danger is that in the great leap from slavery to freedom we may overlook the fact that the masses of us are to live by the productions of our hands, and fail to keep in mind that we shall prosper in proportion as we learn to dignify and glorify common labour and put brains and skill into the common occupations of life; shall prosper in proportion as we learn to draw the line between the superficial and the substantial, the ornamental gewgaws of life and the useful. No race can prosper till it learns that there is as much dignity in tilling a field as in writing a poem. It is at the bottom of life we must begin, and not at the top. Nor should we permit our grievances to overshadow our opportunities.

To those of the white race who look to the incoming of those of foreign birth and strange tongue and habits for the prosperity of the South, were I permitted I would repeat what I say to my own race, "Cast down your bucket where you are." Cast it down among the eight millions of Negroes whose habits you know, whose fidelity and love you have tested in days when to have proved treacherous meant the ruin of your firesides. Cast down your bucket among these people who have, without strikes and labor wars, tilled your fields, cleared your forests, built your railroads and cities, and brought forth treasures from the bowels of the earth, and helped make possible this magnificent representation of the progress of the South. Casting down your bucket among my people, helping and encouraging them as you are doing on these grounds, and to education of head, hand, and heart, you will find that they will buy your surplus land, make blossom the waste places in your fields, and run your factories. While doing this, you can be sure in the future, as in the past, that you and your families will be surrounded by the most patient, faithful, law-abiding, and unresentful people that the world has seen. As we have proved our loyalty to you in the past, in nursing your children, watching by the sick-bed of your mothers and fathers, and often following them with tear-dimmed eyes to their graves, so in the future, in our humble way, we shall stand by you with a devotion that no foreigner can approach, ready to lay down our lives, if need be, in defense of yours, interlacing our industrial, commercial, civil, and religious life with yours in a way that shall make the interests of both races one. In all things that are purely social we can be as separate as the fingers, yet one as the hand in all things essential to mutual progress.

There is no defense or security for any of us except in the highest intelligence and development of all. If anywhere there are efforts tending to curtail the fullest growth of the Negro, let these efforts be turned into stimulating, encouraging, and making him the most useful and intelligent citizen. Effort or means so invested will pay a thousand per cent. interest. These efforts will be twice blessed—"blessing him that gives and him that takes."

There is no escape through law of man or God from the inevitable:

The laws of changeless justice bind Oppressor with oppressed;
And close as sin and suffering joined
We march to fate abreast.

Nearly sixteen millions of hands will aid you in pulling the load upward, or they will pull against you the load downward. We shall constitute one-third and more of the ignorance and crime of the South, or one-third its intelligence and progress; we shall contribute one-third to the business and industrial prosperity of the South, or we shall prove a veritable body of death, stagnating, depressing, retarding every effort to advance the body politic. Gentlemen of the Exposition, as we present to you our humble effort at an exhibition of our progress, you must not expect overmuch. Starting thirty years ago with ownership here and there in a few quilts and pumpkins and chickens (gathered from miscellaneous sources), remember the path that has led from these to the inventions and production of agricultural implements, buggies, steam-engines, newspapers, books, statuary, carving, paintings, the management of drug-stores and banks, has not been trodden without contact with thorns and thistles. While we take pride in what we exhibit as a result of our independent efforts, we do not for a moment forget that our part in this exhibition would fall far short of your expectations but for the constant help that has come to our educational life, not only from the Southern states, but especially from Northern philanthropists, who have made their gifts a constant stream of blessing and encouragement.

The wisest among my race understand that the agitation of questions of social equality is the extremest folly, and that progress in the enjoyment of all the privileges that will come to us must be the result of severe and constant struggle rather than of artificial forcing. No race that has anything to contribute to the markets of the world is long in any degree ostracized.

It is important and right that all privileges of the law be ours, but it is vastly more important that we be prepared for the exercises of these privileges. The opportunity to earn a dollar in a factory just now is worth infinitely more than the opportunity to spend a dollar in an opera-house.

In conclusion, may I repeat that nothing in thirty years has given us more hope and encouragement, and drawn us so near to you of the white race, as this opportunity offered by the Exposition; and here bending, as it were, over the altar that represents the results of the struggles of your race and mine, both starting practically empty-handed three decades ago, I pledge that in your effort to work out the great and intricate problem which God has laid at the doors of the South, you shall have at all times the patient, sympathetic help of my race; only let this be constantly in mind, that, while from representations in these buildings of the product of field, of forest, of mine, of factory, letters, and art, much good will come, yet far above and beyond material benefits will be that higher good, that, let us pray God, will come, in a blotting out of sectional differences and racial animosities and suspicions, in a determination to administer absolute justice, in a willing obedience among all classes to the mandates of law. This, coupled with our material prosperity, will bring into our beloved South a new heaven and a new earth.

Document Thirty

W.E.B. Du Bois Criticizes Booker T. Washington

Context: *W.E.B. Du Bois was one of the most accomplished Americans of the twentieth century. He graduated from Fisk University in 1888 and became the first African American to earn a Ph.D. from Harvard University in 1895. Countering Booker T. Washington's emphasis on industrial education, Du Bois advocated for higher education, especially for the "talented tenth"—exceptional individuals whom he believed would lead African American social, political, and economic uplift. Du Bois had an extraordinary career as a historian and sociologist, eventually writing one of the most important histories of Reconstruction (Black Reconstruction, 1935). Du Bois, however, did not confine himself to the Ivory Tower of academics. He helped start the NAACP and served as an editor of the organization's newspaper* The Crisis *for 24 years. His most well-known book,* The Souls of Black Folk *(1903), reflected both his academic interests and lifelong political activism.*

Questions to Consider: *To what extent did Du Bois's criticisms reflect his own experiences as an accomplished scholar? What did Du Bois see as necessary preconditions for black economic advancement? How did Du Bois define masculinity and how did he use the rhetoric of masculinity to advance his argument? How did Du Bois's critique of Washington's economic program reflect some of the same attitudes toward wealth and accumulation that TR and Jane Addams expressed?*

W.E.B. Du Bois, "Of Mr. Booker T. Washington and Others" (From *The Souls of Black Folk*, 1903)

> *From birth till death enslaved;*
> *in word, in deed, unmanned!*
> *Hereditary bondsmen! Know ye not*
> *Who would be free themselves must strike the blow?*

> BYRON

Easily the most striking thing in the history of the American Negro since 1876 is the ascendancy of Mr. Booker T. Washington. It began at the time when war memories and ideals were rapidly passing; a day of astonishing commercial development was dawning; a sense of doubt and hesitation overtook the freedmen's sons,—then it was that his leading began. Mr. Washington came, with a single definite program, at the psychological moment when the nation was a little ashamed of having bestowed so much sentiment on Negroes, and was concentrating its energies on Dollars. His program of industrial education, conciliation of the South, and submission and silence as to civil and political rights, was not wholly original; the Free Negroes from 1830 up to wartime had striven to build industrial schools, and the American Missionary Association had from the first taught various trades; and Price and others had sought a way of honorable alliance with the best of the Southerners. But Mr. Washington first indissolubly linked these things; he put enthusiasm, unlimited energy, and perfect faith into this program, and changed it from a by-path into a veritable Way of Life. And the tale of the methods by which he did this is a fascinating study of human life.

It startled the nation to hear a Negro advocating such a program after many decades of bitter complaint; it startled and won the applause of the South, it interested and won the admiration of the North; and after a confused murmur of protest, it silenced if it did not convert the Negroes themselves.

To gain the sympathy and cooperation of the various elements comprising the white South was Mr. Washington's first task; and this, at the time Tuskegee was founded, seemed, for a black man, well-nigh impossible. And yet ten years later it was done in the word spoken at Atlanta: "In all things purely social we can be as separate as the five fingers, and yet one as the hand in all things essential to mutual progress." This "Atlanta Compromise" is by all odds the most notable thing in Mr. Washington's career. The South interpreted it in different ways: the radicals received it as a complete surrender of the demand for civil and political equality; the conservatives, as a generously conceived working basis for mutual understanding. So both approved it, and today its author is certainly the most distinguished Southerner since Jefferson Davis, and the one with the largest personal following.

Next to this achievement comes Mr. Washington's work in gaining place and consideration in the North. . . . Mr. Washington knew the heart of the South from birth and training, so by singular insight he intuitively grasped the spirit of the age which was dominating the North. And so thoroughly did he learn the speech and thought of triumphant commercialism, and the ideals of material prosperity that the picture of a lone black boy poring over a French grammar amid the weeds and dirt of a neglected home soon seemed to him the acme of absurdities. One wonders what Socrates and St. Francis of Assisi would say to this.

And yet this very singleness of vision and thorough oneness with his age is a mark of the successful man. It is as though Nature must needs make men narrow in order to give them force. So Mr. Washington's cult has gained unquestioning followers, his work has wonderfully prospered, his friends are legion, and his enemies are confounded. Today he stands as the one recognized spokesman of his ten million fellows, and one of the most notable figures in a nation of seventy millions. One hesitates, therefore, to criticize a life which, beginning with so little has done so much. And yet the time is come when one may speak in all sincerity and utter courtesy of the mistakes and shortcomings of Mr. Washington's career, as well as of his triumphs, without being thought captious or envious, and without forgetting that it is easier to do ill than well in the world.

The criticism that has hitherto met Mr. Washington has not always been of this broad character. In the South especially has he had to walk warily to avoid the harshest judgments,—and naturally so, for he is dealing with the one subject of deepest sensitiveness to that section. Twice—once when at the Chicago celebration of the Spanish-American War he alluded to the color-prejudice that is "eating away the vitals of the South," and once when he dined with President Roosevelt—has the resulting Southern criticism been violent enough to threaten seriously his popularity. In the North the feeling has several times forced itself into words, that Mr. Washington's counsels of submission overlooked certain elements of true manhood, and that his educational program was unnecessarily narrow. Usually, however, such criticism has not found open expression, although, too, the spiritual sons of the Abolitionists have not been prepared to acknowledge that the schools founded before Tuskegee, by men of broad ideals and self-sacrificing spirit, were wholly failures or worthy of ridicule. While, then, criticism has not failed to follow Mr. Washington, yet the prevailing public opinion of the land has been but too willing to deliver the solution of a wearisome problem into his hands, and say, "If that is all you and your race ask, take it."

Among his own people, however, Mr. Washington has encountered the strongest and most lasting opposition, amounting at times to bitterness, and even to-day continuing strong and insistent even though largely silenced in outward expression by the public opinion of the nation. . . . There is among educated and thoughtful colored men in all parts of the land a feeling of deep regret, sorrow, and apprehension at the wide currency and ascendancy which some of Mr. Washington's theories have gained. . . .

Booker T. Washington arose as essentially the leader not of one race but of two—a compromiser between the South, the North, and the Negro. Naturally the Negroes resented, at first bitterly, signs of compromise which surrendered their civil and political rights, even though this was to be exchanged for larger chances of economic development. The rich and dominating North, however, was not only weary of the race problem, but was investing largely in Southern enterprises, and welcomed any method of peaceful cooperation. Thus, by national opinion, the Negroes began to recognize Mr. Washington's leadership; and the voice of criticism was hushed.

Mr. Washington represents in Negro thought the old attitude of adjustment and submission; but adjustment at such a peculiar time as to make his program unique. This is an age of unusual economic development, and Mr. Washington's program naturally takes an economic cast, becoming a gospel of Work and Money to such an extent as apparently almost completely to overshadow the higher aims of life. Moreover, this is an age when the more advanced races are coming in closer contact with the less developed races, and the race-feeling is therefore intensified; and Mr. Washington's program practically accepts the alleged inferiority of the Negro races. Again, in our own land, the reaction from the sentiment of war time has given impetus to race-prejudice against Negroes, and Mr. Washington withdraws many of the high demands of Negroes as men and American citizens. In other periods of intensified prejudice all the Negro's tendency to self-assertion has been called forth; at this period a policy of submission is advocated. In the history of nearly all other races and peoples the doctrine preached at such crises has been that manly self-respect is worth more than lands and houses, and that a people who voluntarily surrender such respect, or cease striving for it, are not worth civilizing.

In answer to this, it has been claimed that the Negro can survive only through submission. Mr. Washington distinctly asks that black people give up, at least for the present, three things,—

First, political power,

Second, insistence on civil rights,

Third, higher education of Negro youth,

—and concentrate all their energies on industrial education, the accumulation of wealth, and the conciliation of the South. This policy has been courageously and insistently advocated for over fifteen years, and has been triumphant for perhaps ten years. As a result of this tender of the palm-branch, what has been the return? In these years there have occurred:

1. The disfranchisement of the Negro.
2. The legal creation of a distinct status of civil inferiority for the Negro.
3. The steady withdrawal of aid from institutions for the higher training of the Negro.

These movements are not, to be sure, direct results of Mr. Washington's teachings; but his propaganda has, without a shadow of doubt, helped their speedier accomplishment. The question then comes: Is it possible, and probable, that nine millions of men can make effective progress in economic lines if they are deprived of political rights, made a servile caste, and allowed only the most meagre chance for developing their exceptional men? If history and reason give any distinct answer to these questions, it is an emphatic No. And Mr. Washington thus faces the triple paradox of his career:

1. He is striving nobly to make Negro artisans business men and property-owners; but it is utterly impossible, under modern competitive methods, for workingmen and property-owners to defend their rights and exist without the right of suffrage.
2. He insists on thrift and self-respect, but at the same time counsels a silent submission to civic inferiority such as is bound to sap the manhood of any race in the long run.
3. He advocates common-school and industrial training, and depreciates institutions of higher learning; but neither the Negro common-schools, nor Tuskegee itself, could remain open a day were it not for teachers trained in Negro colleges, or trained by their graduates.

This triple paradox in Mr. Washington's position is the object of criticism by two classes of colored Americans. One class is spiritually descended from Toussaint the Savior, through Gabriel, Vesey, and Turner, and they represent the attitude of revolt and revenge; they hate the white South blindly and distrust the white race generally, and so far as they agree on definite action, think that the Negro's only hope lies in emigration beyond the borders of the United States. And yet, by the irony of fate, nothing has more effectually made this program seem hopeless than the recent course of the United States toward weaker and darker peoples in the West Indies, Hawaii, and the Philippines,—for where in the world may we go and be safe from lying and brute Force?

The other class of Negroes who cannot agree with Mr. Washington has hitherto said little aloud. They deprecate the sight of scattered counsels, of internal disagreement; and especially they dislike making their just criticism of a useful and earnest man an excuse for a general discharge of venom from small-minded opponents. . . . Such men feel in conscience bound to ask of this nation three things.

1. The right to vote.
2. Civic equality.
3. The education of youth according to ability.

They acknowledge Mr. Washington's invaluable service in counseling patience and courtesy in such demands; they do not ask that ignorant black men vote when ignorant whites are debarred, or that any reasonable restrictions in the suffrage should not be applied; they know that the low social level or the mass of the race is responsible for much discrimination against it, but they also know, and the nation knows, that relentless color-prejudice is more often a cause than a result of the Negro's degradation; they seek the abatement of this relic of barbarism, and not its systematic encouragement and pampering by all agencies of social power from the Associated Press to the Church of Christ. They advocate, with Mr. Washington, a broad system of Negro common schools supplemented by thorough industrial training; but they are surprised that a man of Mr. Washington's insight cannot see that no such educational system ever has rested or can rest on any other basis than that of the well-equipped college and university, and they insist that there is a demand for a few such institutions throughout the South to train the best of the Negro youth as teachers, professional men, and leaders.

This group of men honor Mr. Washington for his attitude of conciliation toward the white South; they accept the "Atlanta Compromise" in its broadest interpretation; they recognize, with him, many signs of promise, many men of high purpose and fair judgment, in this section; they know that no easy task has been laid upon a region already tottering under heavy burdens. But, nevertheless, they insist that the way to truth and right lies in straightforward honesty, not in indiscriminate flattery; in praising those of the South who do well and criticizing uncompromisingly those who do ill; in taking advantage of the opportunities at hand and urging their fellows to do the same, but at the same time in remembering that only a firm adherence to their higher ideals and aspirations will ever keep those ideals within the realm of possibility. They do not expect that the free right to vote, to enjoy civic rights, and to be educated, will come in a moment; they do not expect to see the bias and prejudices of years disappear at the blast of a trumpet; but they are absolutely certain that the way for a people to gain their reasonable rights is not by voluntarily throwing them away and insisting that they do not want them; that the way for a people to gain respect is not by continually belittling and ridiculing themselves; that, on the contrary, Negroes must insist continually, in season and out of season, that voting is necessary to modern manhood, that color discrimination is barbarism, and that black boys need education as well as white boys.

In failing thus to state plainly and unequivocally the legitimate demands of their people, even at the cost of opposing an honored leader, the thinking classes of American Negroes would shirk a heavy responsibility,—a responsibility to themselves, a responsibility to the struggling masses, a responsibility to the darker races of men whose future depends so largely on this American experiment, but especially a responsibility to this nation,—this common Fatherland. It is wrong to encourage a man or a people in evil-doing; it is wrong to aid and abet a national crime simply because it is unpopular not to do so. The growing spirit of kindliness and reconciliation between the North and South after the frightful difference of a generation ago ought to be a source of deep congratulation to all, and especially to those whose mistreatment caused the war; but if that reconciliation is to be marked by the industrial slavery and civic death of those same black men, with permanent legislation into a position of inferiority, then those black men, if they are really men, are called upon by every consideration of patriotism and loyalty to oppose such a course by all civilized methods, even though such opposition involves disagreement with Mr. Booker T. Washington. We have no right to sit silently by while the inevitable seeds are sown for a harvest of disaster to our children, black and white. . . .

Today. . . the attitude of the Southern whites toward the blacks is not, as so many assume, in all cases the same; the ignorant Southerner hates the Negro, the workingmen fear his competition, the money-makers wish to use him as a laborer, some of the educated see a menace in his upward development, while others—usually the sons of the masters—wish to help him to rise. National opinion has enabled this last class to maintain the Negro common schools, and to protect the Negro partially in property, life, and limb. Through the pressure of the money-makers, the Negro is in danger of being reduced to semi-slavery, especially in the country districts; the workingmen, and those of the educated who fear the Negro, have united to disfranchise him, and some have urged his deportation; while the passions of the ignorant are easily aroused to lynch and abuse any black man. . . .

It would be unjust to Mr. Washington not to acknowledge that in several instances he has opposed movements in the South which were unjust to the Negro; he sent memorials to the Louisiana and Alabama constitutional conventions, he has spoken against lynching, and in other ways has openly or silently set his influence against sinister schemes and unfortunate happenings. Notwithstanding this, it is equally true to assert that on the whole the distinct impression left by Mr. Washington's propaganda is, first, that the South is justified in its present attitude toward the Negro because of the Negro's degradation; secondly, that the prime cause of the Negro's failure to rise more quickly is his wrong education in the past; and, thirdly, that his future rise depends primarily on his own efforts. Each of these propositions is a dangerous half-truth. The supplementary truths must never be lost sight of: first, slavery and race-prejudice are potent if not sufficient causes of the Negro's position; second, industrial and common-school training were necessarily slow in planting because they had to await the black teachers trained by higher institutions. . . and, third, while it is a great truth to say that the Negro must strive and strive mightily to help himself, it is equally true that unless his striving be not simply seconded, but rather aroused and encouraged, by the initiative of the richer and wiser environing group, he cannot hope for great success.

In his failure to realize and impress this last point, Mr. Washington is especially to be criticized. His doctrine has tended to make the whites, North and South, shift the burden of the Negro problem to the Negro's shoulders and stand aside as critical and rather pessimistic spectators; when in fact the burden belongs to the nation, and the hands of none of us are clean if we bend not our energies to righting these great wrongs.

The South ought to be led, by candid and honest criticism, to assert her better self and do her full duty to the race she has cruelly wronged and is still wronging. The North—her co-partner in guilt—cannot salve her conscience by plastering it with gold. We cannot settle this problem by diplomacy and suaveness, by "policy" alone. If worse comes to worst, can the moral fibre of this country survive the slow throttling and murder of nine millions of men?

The black men of America have a duty to perform, a duty stern and delicate,—a forward movement to oppose a part of the work of their greatest leader. So far as Mr. Washington preaches Thrift, Patience, and Industrial Training for the masses, we must hold up his hands and strive with him, rejoicing in his honors and glorying in the strength of this Joshua called of God and of man to lead the headless host. But so far as Mr. Washington apologizes for injustice, North or South, does not rightly value the privilege and duty of voting, belittles the emasculating effects of caste distinctions, and opposes the higher training and ambition of our brighter minds—so far as he, the South, or the Nation, does this—we must unceasingly and firmly oppose them. By every civilized and peaceful method we must strive for the rights which the world accords to men, clinging unwaveringly to those great words which the sons of the Fathers would fain forget: "We hold these truths to be self-evident: That all men are created equal; that they are endowed by their Creator with certain unalienable rights; that among these are life, liberty, and the pursuit of happiness."

Ida B. Wells Condemns Lynching

Context: *Lynching had been part of southern life for several generations, but in the 1890s it reached epidemic proportions. Between 1890 and 1910, nearly 100 blacks were lynched every year. Ida B. Wells was one of the nation's most outspoken critics of lynching. Born a slave in 1862, Wells became a school teacher and civil rights leader in Memphis, Tennessee. When a white mob lynched three of her friends in 1892, she helped organize a black boycott of white-owned businesses and wrote scathing editorials in her own newspaper. After a mob ransacked her newspaper office, she left Memphis and eventually settled in Chicago. Her best known publication was* Southern Horrors: Lynch Law in All Its Phases *(1892).*

Questions to Consider: *Why did Wells stress that lynching was a national problem, instead of merely a regional one? Why did Wells argue that rape was not the alleged offense in most lynchings? What pragmatic reasons did Wells give for ending lynching? How did Wells use the rhetoric of manliness and civilization to advance her anti-lynching crusade? How did her rhetoric try to win the support of white Americans? How did Wells's strategy for mobilizing the support of whites compare to Booker T. Washington's tactics?*

Ida B. Wells, "Lynch Law in America" (1900)

Our country's national crime is *lynching*. It is not the creature of an hour, the sudden outburst of uncontrolled fury, or the unspeakable brutality of an insane mob. It represents the cool, calculating deliberation of intelligent people who openly avow that there is an "unwritten law" that justifies them in putting human beings to death without complaint under oath, without trial by jury, without opportunity to make defense, and without right of appeal. . . . No emergency called for lynch law. It asserted its sway in defiance of law and in favor of anarchy. . . . In the thirty years of its existence [it has marked] the inhuman butchery of more than ten thousand men, women, and children by shooting, drowning, hanging, and burning them alive. Not only this, but so potent is the force of example that the lynching mania has spread throughout the North and middle West. It is now no uncommon thing to read of lynchings north of Mason and Dixon's line, and those most responsible for this fashion gleefully point to these instances and assert that the North is no better than the South.

This is the work of the "unwritten law" about which so much is said, and in whose behest butchery is made a pastime and national savagery condoned. The first statute of this "unwritten law" was written in the blood of thousands of brave men who thought that a government that was good enough to create a citizenship was strong enough to protect it. Under the authority of a national law that gave every citizen the right to vote, the newly-made citizens chose to exercise their suffrage. But the reign of the national law was short-lived and illusionary. Hardly had the sentences dried upon the statute-books before one Southern State after another raised the cry against "negro domination" and proclaimed there was an "unwritten law" that justified any means to resist it.

The method then inaugurated was the outrages by the "red-shirt" bands of Louisiana, South Carolina, and other Southern States, which were succeeded by the Ku-Klux Klans. These advocates of the "unwritten law" boldly avowed their purpose to intimidate, suppress, and nullify the negro's right to vote. In support of its plans the Ku-Klux Klans, the "red-shirt" and similar organizations proceeded to beat, exile, and kill negroes until the purpose of their organization was accomplished and the supremacy of the "unwritten law" was effected. Thus lynchings began in the South, rapidly spreading into the various States until the national law was nullified and the reign of the "unwritten law" was supreme. Men were taken from their homes by "red-shirt" bands and stripped, beaten, and exiled; others were assassinated when their political prominence made them obnoxious to their political opponents; while the Ku-Klux barbarism of election days, reveling in the butchery of thousands of colored voters, furnished records in Congressional investigations that are a disgrace to civilization.

The alleged menace of universal suffrage having been avoided by the absolute suppression of the negro vote, the spirit of mob murder should have been satisfied and the butchery of negroes should have ceased. But men, women, and children were the victims of murder by individuals and murder by mobs, just as they had been when killed at the demands of the "unwritten law" to prevent "negro domination." Negroes were killed for disputing over terms of contracts with their employers. If a few barns were burned some colored man was killed to stop it. If a colored man resented the imposition of a white man and the two came to blows, the colored man had to die, either at the hands of the white man then and there or later at the hands of a mob that speedily gathered. If he showed a spirit of courageous manhood he was hanged for his pains, and the killing was justified by the declaration that he was a "saucy nigger." Colored women have been murdered because they refused to tell the mobs where relatives could be found for "lynching bees." Boys of fourteen years have been lynched by white representatives of American civilization. In fact, for all kinds of offenses—and, for no offenses—from murders to misdemeanors, men and women are put to death without judge or jury; so that, although the political excuse was no longer necessary, the wholesale murder of human beings went on just the same. A new name was given to the killings and a new excuse was invented for so doing.

Again the aid of the "unwritten law" is invoked, and again it comes to the rescue. During the last ten years a new statute has been added to the "unwritten law." This statute proclaims that for certain crimes or alleged crimes no negro shall be allowed a trial; that no white woman shall be compelled to charge an assault under oath or to submit any such charge to the investigation of a court of law. The result is that many men have been put to death whose innocence was afterward established; and to-day, under this reign of the "unwritten law," no colored man, no matter what his reputation, is safe from lynching if a white woman, no matter what her standing or motive, cares to charge him with insult or assault. . . . No matter that our laws presume every man innocent until he is proved guilty; no matter that it leaves a certain class of individuals completely at the mercy of another class; no matter that it encourages those criminally disposed to blacken their faces and commit any crime in the calendar so long as they can throw suspicion on some negro, as is frequently done, and then lead a mob to take his life; no matter that mobs make a farce of the law and a mockery of justice; no matter that hundreds of boys are being hardened in crime and schooled in vice by the repetition of such scenes before their eyes—if a white woman declares herself insulted or assaulted, some life must pay the penalty, with all the horrors of the Spanish Inquisition and all the barbarism of the Middle Ages. The world looks on and says it is well.

Not only are two hundred men and women put to death annually, on the average, in this country by mobs, but these lives are taken with the greatest publicity. In many instances the leading citizens aid and abet by their presence when they do not participate, and the leading journals inflame the public mind to the lynching point with scare-head articles and offers of rewards. Whenever a burning is advertised to take place, the railroads run excursions, photographs are taken, and the same jubilee is indulged in that characterized the public hangings of one hundred years ago. There is, however, this difference: in those old days the multitude that stood by was permitted only to guy or jeer. The nineteenth century lynching mob cuts off ears, toes, and fingers, strips off flesh, and distributes portions of the body as souvenirs among the crowd. If the leaders of the mob are so minded, coal-oil is poured over the body and the victim is then roasted to death. This has been done in Texarkana and Paris, Tex., in Bardswell, Ky., and in Newman, Ga. In Paris the officers of the law delivered the prisoner to the mob. The mayor gave the school children a holiday and the railroads ran excursion trains so that the people might see a human being burned to death. In Texarkana, the year before, men and boys amused themselves by cutting off strips of flesh and thrusting knives into their helpless victim. At Newman, Ga., of the present year, the mob tried every conceivable torture to compel the victim to cry out and confess, before they set fire to the faggots that burned him. But their trouble was all in vain—he never uttered a cry, and they could not make him confess.

This condition of affairs were brutal enough and horrible enough if it were true that lynchings occurred only because of the commission of crimes against women—as is constantly declared by ministers, editors, lawyers, teachers, statesmen, and even by women themselves.

It has been to the interest of those who did the lynching to blacken the good name of the helpless and defenseless victims of their hate. For this reason they publish at every possible opportunity this excuse for lynching, hoping thereby not only to palliate their own crime but at the same time to prove the negro a moral monster and unworthy of the respect and sympathy of the civilized world. But this alleged reason adds to the deliberate injustice of the mob's work. Instead of lynchings being caused by assaults upon women, the statistics show that not one-third of the victims of lynchings are even charged with such crimes.

Indeed, the record for the last twenty years shows exactly the same or a smaller proportion who have been charged with this horrible crime. Quite a number of the one-third alleged cases of assault that have been personally investigated by the writer have shown that there was no foundation in fact for the charges; yet the claim is not made that there were no real culprits among them. The negro has been too long associated with the white man not to have copied his vices as well as his virtues. But the negro resents and utterly repudiates the efforts to blacken his good name by asserting that assaults upon women are peculiar to his race. The negro has suffered far more from the commission of this crime against the women of his race by white men than the white race has ever suffered through *his* crimes. Very scant notice is taken of the matter when this is the condition of affairs. What becomes a crime deserving capital punishment when the tables are turned is a matter of small moment when the negro woman is the accusing party.

But since the world has accepted this false and unjust statement, and the burden of proof has been placed upon the negro to vindicate his race, he is taking steps to do so. The Anti-Lynching Bureau of the National Afro-American Council is arranging to have every lynching investigated and publish the facts to the world. . . . All the negro asks is justice—a fair and impartial trial in the courts of the country. That given, he will abide the result.

But this question affects the entire American nation, and from several points of view: First, on the ground of consistency. Our watchword has been "the land of the free and the home of the brave." Brave men do not gather by thousands to torture and murder a single individual, so gagged and bound he cannot make even feeble resistance or defense. Neither do brave men or women stand by and see such things done without compunction of conscience, nor read of them without protest. . . . Surely it should be the nation's duty to correct its own evils!

Second, on the ground of economy. To those who fail to be convinced from any other point of view touching this momentous question, a consideration of the economic phase might not be amiss. It is generally known that mobs in Louisiana, Colorado, Wyoming, and other States have lynched subjects of other countries. . . . The United States already has paid in indemnities for lynching nearly a half million dollars.

Third, for the honor of Anglo-Saxon civilization. No scoffer at our boasted American civilization could say anything more harsh of it than does the American white man himself who says he is unable to protect the honor of his women without resort to such brutal, inhuman, and degrading exhibitions as characterize "lynching bees." The cannibals of the South Sea Islands roast human beings alive to satisfy hunger. The red Indian of the Western plains tied his prisoner to the stake, tortured him, and danced in fiendish glee while his victim writhed in the flames. His savage, untutored mind suggested no better way than that of wreaking vengeance upon those who had wronged him. These people knew nothing about Christianity and did not profess to follow its teachings; but such primary laws as they had they lived up to. No nation, savage or civilized, save only the United States of America, has confessed its inability to protect its women save by hanging, shooting, and burning alleged offenders.

Finally, for love of country. No American travels abroad without blushing for shame for his country on this subject. And whatever the excuse that passes current in the United States, it avails nothing abroad. With all the powers of government in control; with all laws made by white men, administered by white judges, jurors, prosecuting attorneys, and sheriffs; with every office of the executive department filled by white men—no excuse can be offered for exchanging the orderly administration of justice for barbarous lynchings and "unwritten laws." Our country should be placed speedily above the plane of confessing herself a failure at self-government. This cannot be until Americans of every section, of broadest patriotism and best and wisest citizenship, not only see the defect in our country's armor but take the necessary steps to remedy it. Although lynchings have steadily increased in number and barbarity during the last twenty years, there has been no single effort put forth by the many moral and philanthropic forces of the country to put a stop to this wholesale slaughter. Indeed, the silence grows more marked as the years go by.

Name: _____ Date: _____

Document Analysis Worksheet

1. Date/Author of Document/Author's Position: Intended Audience:

2. Why was this document written? List three points the author made that you find important.

3. List two things the document tells you about life in the United States at the time it was written.

4. Write a question to the author that the document left unanswered.

Comparative Analysis Worksheet

Choose two documents from this week's readings in which the document authors present different takes on a particular issue.

  1. Identify two or three key points on which the authors agree and/or disagree.

_____

_____

_____

_____

_____

_____

_____

  2. Develop your analysis of these two documents further by answering one or two questions listed in the "Questions to Consider" section for each document.

_____

_____

_____

_____

_____

_____

_____

_____

_____

_____

_____

Document Thirty-Two

Elizabeth Cady Stanton Justifies Complete Equality

Context: *Elizabeth Cady Stanton had been a leader of the suffrage movement for more than forty years when she delivered the address "The Solitude of Self" (1892). Stanton had become increasingly isolated within the women's rights movement. While she continued to advocate a radical agenda of complete equality, most suffrage leaders wanted to focus exclusively on suffrage. To their eyes, Stanton's radical stands were more of a hindrance than a help. Stanton resigned from the presidency of the major suffrage organization after giving this address.*

Questions to Consider: *What were Stanton's justifications for women's equality? What are the connections, if any, between "The Solitude of Self" and Stanton's ideals expressed at the Seneca Falls convention? To what extent was Stanton's message outside the main currents of Progressive ideology? How would have William Graham Sumner and Andrew Carnegie reacted to this speech?*

Elizabeth Cady Stanton, "The Solitude of Self" (1892)

(Address Delivered by Mrs. Stanton Before the Committee of the Judiciary of the United States Congress Monday, January 18, 1892).

The point I wish plainly to bring before you on this occasion is the individuality of each human soul; our Protestant idea, the right of individual conscience and judgment—our republican idea, individual citizenship. In discussing the rights of woman, we are to consider, first, what belongs to her as an individual, in a world of her own, the arbiter of her own destiny, an imaginary Robinson Crusoe with her woman Friday on a solitary island. Her rights under such circumstances are to use all her faculties for her own safety and happiness.

Secondly, if we consider her as a citizen, as a member of a great nation, she must have the same rights as all other members, according to the fundamental principles of our Government.

Thirdly, viewed as a woman, an equal factor in civilization, her rights and duties are still the same—individual happiness and development.

Fourthly, it is only the incidental relations of life, such as mother, wife, sister, daughter, that may involve some special duties and training. In the usual discussion in regard to woman's sphere, such men as Herbert Spencer, Frederic Harrison, and Grant Allen uniformly subordinate her rights and duties as an individual, as a citizen, as a woman, to the necessities of these incidental relations, some of which a large class of woman may never assume. In discussing the sphere of man we do not decide his rights as an individual, as a citizen, as a man by his duties as a father, a husband, a brother, or a son, relations some of which he may never fill. Moreover he would be better fitted for these very relations and whatever special work he might choose to do to earn his bread by the complete development of all his faculties as an individual.

Just so with woman. The education that will fit her to discharge the duties in the largest sphere of human usefulness will best fit her for whatever special work she may be compelled to do.

The isolation of every human soul and the necessity of self-dependence must give each individual the right, to choose his own surroundings.

The strongest reason for giving woman all the opportunities for higher education, for the full development of her faculties, forces of mind and body; for giving her the most enlarged freedom of thought and action; a complete emancipation from all forms of bondage, of custom, dependence, superstition; from all the crippling influences of fear, is the solitude and personal responsibility of her own individual life. The strongest reason why we ask for woman a voice in the government under which she lives; in the religion she is asked to believe; equality in social life, where she is the chief factor; a place in the trades and professions, where she may earn her bread, is because of her birthright to self-sovereignty; because, as an individual, she must rely on herself. No matter how much women prefer to lean, to be protected and supported, nor how much men desire to have them do so, they must make the voyage of life alone, and for safety in an emergency they must know something of the laws of navigation. To guide our own craft, we must be captain, pilot, engineer; with chart and compass to stand at the wheel; to match the wind and waves and know when to take in the sail, and to read the signs in the firmament over all. It matters not whether the solitary voyager is man or woman.

Nature having endowed them equally, leaves them to their own skill and judgment in the hour of danger, and, if not equal to the occasion, alike they perish.

To appreciate the importance of fitting every human soul for independent action, think for a moment of the immeasurable solitude of self. We come into the world alone, unlike all who have gone before us; we leave it alone under circumstances peculiar to ourselves. No mortal ever has been, no mortal ever will be like the soul just launched on the sea of life. . . .

In hours like these we realize the awful solitude of individual life, its pains, its penalties, its responsibilities; hours in which the youngest and most helpless are thrown on their own resources for guidance and consolation. Seeing then that life must ever be a march and a battle, that each soldier must be equipped for his own protection, it is the height of cruelty to rob the individual of a single natural right.

To throw obstacle in the way of a complete education is like putting out the eyes; to deny the rights of property, like cutting off the hands. To deny political equality is to rob the ostracized of all self-respect; of credit in the market place; of recompense in the world of work; of a voice among those who make and administer the law; a choice in the jury before whom they are tried, and in the judge who decides their punishment. . . . Robbed of her natural rights, handicapped by law and custom at every turn, yet compelled to fight her own battles, and in the emergencies of life to fall back on herself for protection. . . .

The young wife and mother, at the head of some establishment with a kind husband to shield her from the adverse winds of life, with wealth, fortune and position, has a certain harbor of safety, secure against the ordinary ills of life. But to manage a household, have an influence in society, keep her friends and the affections of her husband, train her children and servants well, she must have rare common sense, wisdom, diplomacy, and a knowledge of human nature. To do all this she needs the cardinal virtues and the strong points of character that the most successful statesman possesses.

An uneducated woman, trained to dependence, with no resources in herself must make a failure of any position in life. But society says women do not need a knowledge of the world, the liberal training that experience in public life must give, all the advantages of collegiate education; but when for the lack of all this, the woman's happiness is wrecked, alone she bears her humiliation; and the attitude of the weak and the ignorant is indeed pitiful in the wild chase for the prizes of life they are ground to powder.

In age, when the pleasures of youth are passed, children grown up, married and gone, the hurry and hustle of life in a measure over, when the hands are weary of active service, when the old armchair and the fireside are the chosen resorts, then men and women alike must fall back on their own resources. If they cannot find companionship in books, if they have no interest in the vital questions of the hour, no interest in watching the consummation of reforms, with which they might have been identified, they soon pass into their dotage. The more fully the faculties of the mind are developed and kept in use, the longer the period of vigor and active interest in all around us continues. If from a lifelong participation in public affairs a woman feels responsible for the laws regulating our system of education, the discipline of our jails and prisons, the sanitary conditions of our private homes, public buildings, and thoroughfares, an interest in commerce, finance, our foreign relations, in any or all of these questions, here solitude will at least be respectable, and she will not be driven to gossip or scandal for entertainment. . . .

Whatever the theories may be of woman's dependence on man, in the supreme moments of her life he can not bear her burdens. Alone she goes to the gates of death to give life to every man that is born into the world. No one can share her fears, no one mitigate her pangs; and if her sorrow is greater than she can bear, alone she passes beyond the gates into the vast unknown. . . .

But when. . .women are recognized as individuals, responsible for their own environments, thoroughly educated for all the positions in life they may be called to fill; with all the resources in themselves that liberal thought and broad culture can give; guided by their own conscience and judgment; trained to self-protection by a healthy development of the muscular system and skill in the use of weapons of defense, and stimulated to self-support by the knowledge of the business world and the pleasure that pecuniary independence must ever give; when women are trained in this way they will, in a measure, be fitted for those hours of solitude that come alike to all, whether prepared or otherwise. As in our extremity we must depend on ourselves, the dictates of wisdom point to complete individual development. . . .

Whatever may be said of man's protecting power in ordinary conditions, amid all the terrible disasters by land and sea, in the supreme moments of danger, alone, woman must ever meet the horrors of the situation; the Angel of Death even makes no royal pathway for her. Man's love and sympathy enter only into the sunshine of our lives. In that solemn solitude of self, that links us with the immeasurable and the eternal, each soul lives alone forever. . . . Who, I ask you, can take, dare take on himself the rights, the duties, the responsibilities of another human soul?

Document Thirty-Three

Jane Addams Extends Domestic Ideology to Municipal Government

Context: *Like many settlement house residents, Jane Addams was a strong proponent of women's rights, especially suffrage. While some supporters of suffrage used racial arguments to justify their position—the votes of white women would offset the votes of blacks and immigrants—Addams had a more inclusive vision of suffrage.*

Questions to Consider: *What general ideas and attitudes did Addams use to justify suffrage? How did Addams use her Hull House experience to shape her arguments? How did Addams's arguments for suffrage differ from those of Elizabeth Cady Stanton? To what extent did Addams argue that men and women were inherently different in their political outlooks? How could domestic ideology both strengthen and weaken arguments for suffrage?*

Jane Addams, "Why Women Should Vote" (1915)

Reprinted in *Woman Suffrage: History, Arguments, and Results* (New York: National Woman Suffrage Publishing Co., Revised Edition, May, 1917).

For many generations it has been believed that woman's place is within the walls of her own home, and it is indeed impossible to imagine the time when her duty there shall be ended or to forecast any social change which shall release her from that paramount obligation. This paper is an attempt to show that many women to-day are failing to discharge their duties to their own households properly simply because they do not perceive that as society grows more complicated it is necessary that woman shall extend her sense of responsibility to many things outside of her own home if she would continue to preserve the home in its entirety. One could illustrate in many ways. A woman's simplest duty, one would say, is to keep her house clean and wholesome, and to feed her children properly. Yet if she lives in a tenement house, as so many of my neighbors do, she cannot fulfill these simple obligations by her own efforts because she is utterly dependent upon the city administration for the conditions which render decent living possible. Her basement will not be dry, her stairways will not be fireproof, her house will not be provided with sufficient windows to give light and air, nor will it be equipped with sanitary plumbing, unless the Public Works Department sends inspectors who constantly insist that these elementary decencies be provided. Women who live in the country sweep their own dooryards and may either feed the refuse of the table to a flock of chickens or allow it innocently to decay in the open air and sunshine. In a crowded city quarter, however, if the street is not cleaned by the city authorities, no amount of private sweeping will keep the tenement free from grime; if the garbage is not properly collected and destroyed, a tenement house mother may see her children sicken and die of diseases from which she alone is powerless to shield them, although her tenderness and devotion are unbounded. She cannot even secure untainted meat for her household, she cannot provide fresh fruit, unless the meat has been inspected by city officials, and the decayed fruit, which is so often placed upon sale in the tenement districts, has been destroyed in the interests of public health. In short, if woman would keep on with her old business of caring for her house and rearing her children, she will have to have some conscience in regard to public affairs lying quite outside of her immediate household. The individual conscience and devotion are no longer effective.

Chicago one spring had a spreading contagion of scarlet fever just at the time that the school nurses had been discontinued because business men had pronounced them too expensive. If the women who sent their children to the schools had been sufficiently public-spirited and had been provided with an implement through which to express that public spirit, they would have insisted that the schools be supplied with nurses in order that their own children might be protected from contagion. In other words, if women would effectively continue their old avocations they must take part in the slow upbuilding of that code of legislation which is alone sufficient to protect the home from the dangers incident to modern life. One might instance the many deaths of children from contagious diseases the germs of which had been carried in tailored clothing. . . from infected city sweatshops. That their mothers mend their stockings and guard them from "taking cold" is not a sufficient protection, when the tailoring of the family is done in a distant city under conditions which the mother cannot possibly control. The sanitary regulation of sweatshops by city officials is all that can be depended upon to prevent such needless destruction. Who shall say that women are not concerned in the enactment and enforcement of such legislation if they would preserve their homes? . . .

One of the interesting experiences in the Chicago campaign for inducing the members of the Charter Convention to recommend municipal franchise for women in the provisions of the new charter was the unexpected enthusiasm and help which came from large groups of foreign-born women. The Scandinavian women represented in many Lutheran Church societies said quite simply that in the old country they had had the municipal franchise upon the same basis as men for many years; all the women living under the British Government, in England, Australia or Canada, pointed out that Chicago women were asking now for what the British women had long ago. But the most unexpected response came from the foreign colonies in which women had never heard such problems discussed, and took the prospect of the municipal ballot as a simple device—which it is—to aid them in their daily struggle with adverse city conditions. . . .

. . . If women follow only the lines of their traditional activities, here are certain primary duties which belong to even the most conservative women, and which no one woman or group of women can adequately discharge unless they join the more general movements looking toward social amelioration through legal enactment.

The first of these, of which this article has already treated, is woman's responsibility for the members of her own household that they may be properly fed and clothed and surrounded by hygienic conditions. The second is a responsibility for the education of children: (a) that they may be provided with good books; (b) that they may be kept free from vicious influences on the street; (c) that when working they may be protected by adequate child-labor legislation.

(a) The duty of a woman toward the schools which her children attend is so obvious that it is not necessary to dwell upon it. But even this simple obligation cannot be effectively carried out without some form of social organization, as the mothers school clubs and mothers congresses testify, and to which the most conservative women belong because they feel the need of wider reading and discussion concerning the many problems of childhood. It is, therefore, perhaps natural that the public should have been more willing to accord a vote to women in school matters than in any other, and yet women have never been members of a Board of Education in sufficient numbers to influence largely actual school curriculi. If they had been kindergartens, domestic science courses and school playgrounds would be far more numerous than they are. More than one woman has been convinced of the need of the ballot by the futility of her efforts in persuading a business man that young children need nurture in something besides the three r's. Perhaps, too, only women realize the influence which the school might exert upon the home if a proper adaptation to actual needs were considered. An Italian girl who has had lessons in cooking at the public school will help her mother to connect the entire family with American food and household habits. . . .

As a result of this teaching I recall a young girl who carefully explained to her Italian mother that the reason the babies in Italy were so healthy and the babies in Chicago were so sickly was not, as her mother had always firmly insisted, because her babies in Italy had goat's milk and her babies in America had cow's milk, but because the milk in Italy was clean and the milk in Chicago was dirty. She said that when you milked your own goat before the door you knew that the milk was clean, but when you bought milk from the grocery store after it had been carried for many miles in the country, "you couldn't tell whether or not it was fit for baby to drink until the men from the City Hall, who had watched it all the way, said that it was all right." She also informed her mother that the "City Hall wanted to fix up the milk so that it couldn't make the baby sick, but that they hadn't quite enough votes for it yet."

. . .(b) women are also beginning to realize that children need attention outside of school hours; that much of the petty vice in cities is merely the love of pleasure gone wrong, the over-restrained boy or girl seeking improper recreation and excitement. It is obvious that a little study of the needs of children, a sympathetic understanding of the conditions under which they go astray, might save hundreds of them. Women traditionally have had an opportunity to observe the plays of children and the needs of youth, and yet in Chicago, at least, they had done singularly little in this vexed problem of juvenile delinquency until they helped to inaugurate the Juvenile Court movement a dozen years ago. The Juvenile Court Committee, made up largely of women, paid the salaries of the probation officers connected with the court for the first six years of its existence, and after the salaries were cared for by the county the same organization turned itself into a Juvenile Protective League, and through a score of paid officers are doing valiant service in minimizing some of the dangers of city life which boys and girls encounter.

This Protective League, however, was not formed until the women had had a civic training through their semi-official connection with the Juvenile Court. . . . We would all agree that social amelioration must come about through the efforts of many people who are moved thereto by the compunction and stirring of the individual conscience, but we are only begin-ning to understand that the individual conscience will respond to the special challenge largely in proportion as the individual is able to see the social conditions because he has felt respon-sible for their improvement. Because this body of women assumed a public responsibility they have seen to it that every series of pictures displayed in the five-cent theatre is subjected to a careful censorship before it is produced, and those series suggesting obscenity and crimi-nality have been practically eliminated. The police department has performed this and many other duties to which it was oblivious before, simply because these women have made it real-ize that it is necessary to protect and purify those places of amusement which are crowded with young people every night. . . . The more extensively the modern city endeavors on the one hand to control and on the other hand to provide recreational facilities for its young people, the more necessary it is that women should assist in their direction and extension. After all, a care for wholesome and innocent amusement is what women have for many years assumed. When the reaction comes on the part of taxpayers, women's votes may be necessary to keep the city to its beneficent obligations towards its own young people.

(c) As the education of her children has been more and more transferred to the school, so that even children four years old go to the kindergarten, the woman has been left in a household of constantly narrowing interests, not only because the children are away, but also because one industry after another is slipping from the household into the factory. Ever since steam power has been applied to the processes of weaving and spinning woman's traditional work has been carried on largely outside of the home. . . . Because many thousands of those work-ing in factories and shops are girls between the ages of fourteen and twenty-two, there is a necessity that older women should be interested in the conditions of industry. The very fact that these girls are not going to remain in industry permanently makes it more important that some one should see to it that they shall not be incapacitated for their future family life because they work for exhausting hours and under unsanitary conditions.

If woman's sense of obligation had enlarged as the industrial condition changed, she might naturally and almost imperceptibly have inaugurated the movements for social amelioration in the line of factory legislation and shop sanitation. That she has not done so is doubtless due to the fact that her conscience is slow to recognize any obligation outside of her own family circle, and because she was so absorbed in her own household that she failed to see what the conditions outside actually were. . . .

. . . [M]any busy women would be glad to use the ballot to further public measures in which they are interested and for which they have been working for years. It offends the taste of such a woman to be obliged to use indirect "influence" when she is accustomed to well-bred, open action in other affairs, and she very much resents the time spent in persuading a voter to take her point of view, and possibly to give up his own quite as honest and valuable as hers, although different because resulting from a totally different experience. Public-spirited women who wish to use the ballot, as I know them, do not wish to do the work of men nor to take over men's affairs. They simply want an opportunity to do their own work and to take care of those affairs which naturally and historically belong to women, but which are constantly being overlooked and slighted in our political institutions. . . .

To turn the administration of our civic affairs wholly over to men may mean that the American city will continue to push forward in its commercial and industrial development, and continue to lag behind in those things which make a city healthful and beautiful. After all, woman's traditional function has been to make her dwelling-place both clean and fair. Is that dreariness in city life, that lack of domesticity which the humblest farm dwelling presents, due to a withdrawal of one of the naturally co-operating forces? If women have in any sense been responsible for the gentler side of life which softens and blurs some of its harsher conditions, may they not have a duty to perform in our American cities?

In closing, may I recapitulate that if woman would fulfill her traditional responsibility to her own children; if she would educate and protect from danger factory children who must find their recreation on the street; if she would bring the cultural forces to bear upon our materialistic civilization; and if she would do it all with the dignity and directness fitting one who carries on her immemorial duties, then she must bring herself to the use of the ballot—that latest implement for self-government. May we not fairly say the American women need this implement in order to preserve the home?

Belle Kearney Equates Suffrage with White Supremacy

Context: *The women's suffrage movement originated from the abolitionist agitation of the 1830s and 1840s. Recall that African-American abolitionist Frederick Douglass eloquently spoke on behalf of women's suffrage at the 1848 Seneca Falls convention. By the Progressive period, though, the orientation of the movement had changed. While some suffrage supporters still advocated complete equality of all races, others argued that the greater propensity of white women to vote would effectively dilute the political power of immigrants and African Americans. Belle Kearney, a white Mississippi suffragist who addressed the 1903 NAWSA convention, typified racist appeals for women's suffrage.*

Questions to Consider: *How, according to Kearney, would women's suffrage help maintain white supremacy in the South? Why would women's suffrage help stimulate progress among poor whites? Why did Kearney consider the Tuskegee Institute and other black vocational schools a threat to white supremacy? From the standpoint of practical politics, did Kearney's embrace of racism ultimately help or hurt the suffrage cause?*

Belle Kearney, "The South and Woman Suffrage," (1903)

By degrees, slavery became the bone of contention in politics. In course of time it would probably have been abolished by the Southerners themselves, if they had been left to work out their own destiny and that of the black man in bonds, but a conflict of ideas gathered to a storm-center between the Puritan of the North and the Cavalier of the South, and the institution was wiped out in blood.

The world is scarcely beginning to realize the enormity of the situation that faces the South in its grapple with the race question which was thrust upon it at the close of the Civil War, when 4,500,000 ex-slaves, illiterate and semi-barbarous, were enfranchised. Such a situation has no parallel in history. In forging a path out of the darkness, there were no precedents to lead the way. All that has been and is being accomplished is pioneer statecraft. The South has struggled under its death-weight for nearly forty years, bravely and magnanimously.

The Southern States are making a desperate effort to maintain the political supremacy of Anglo-Saxonism by amendments to their constitutions limiting the right to vote by a property and educational qualification. If the United States government had been wise enough to enact such a law when the negro was first enfranchised, it would have saved years of bloodshed in the South, and such experiences of suffering and horror among the white people here as no other were ever subjected to in an enlightened nation.

The present suffrage laws in the different Southern States can be only temporary measures for protection. Those who are wise enough to look beneath the surface will be compelled to realize the fact that they act as a stimulus to the black man to acquire both education and property, but no incentive is given to the poor whites; for it is understood, in a general way, that any man whose skin is fair enough to let the blue veins show through, may be allowed the right of franchise.

The industrial education that the negro is receiving at Tuskegee and other schools is only fitting him for power, and when the black man becomes necessary to a community by reason of his skill and acquired wealth, and the poor white man, embittered by his poverty and humiliated by his inferiority, finds no place for himself or his children, then will come the grapple between the races.

To avoid this unspeakable culmination, the enfranchisement of women will have to be effected, and an educational and property qualification for the ballot be made to apply, without discrimination, to both sexes and to both races. It will spur the poor white to keep up with the march of progression, and enable him to hold his own. The class that is not willing to measure its strength with that of an inferior is not fit to survive.

The enfranchisement of women would insure immediate and durable white supremacy, honestly attained; for, upon unquestionable authority, it is stated that "in every Southern State but one, there are more educated women than all the illiterate voters, white and black, native and foreign, combined." As you probably know, of all the women in the South who can read and write, ten out of every eleven are white. When it comes to the proportion of property between the races, that of the white outweighs that of the black immeasurably. The South is slow to grasp the great fact that the enfranchisement of women would settle the race question in politics.

The civilization of the North is threatened by the influx of foreigners with their imported customs; by the greed of monopolistic wealth, and the unrest among the working classes; by the strength of the liquor traffic, and by encroachments upon religious belief.

Some day the North will be compelled to look to the South for redemption from these evils, on account of the purity of its Anglo-Saxon blood, the simplicity of its social and economic structure, the great advance in prohibitory law, and the maintenance of the sanctity of its faith, which has been kept inviolate. Just as surely as the North will be forced to turn to the South for the nation's salvation, just so surely will the South be compelled to look to its Anglo-Saxon women as the medium through which to retain the supremacy of the white race over the African. . . .

Anglo-Saxonism is the standard of the ages to come. It is, above all else, the granite foundation of the South. Upon that its civilization will mount; upon that it will stand unshaken. . . . Thank God the black man was freed! I wish for him all possible happiness and all possible progress, but not in encroachments upon the holy of holies of the Anglo-Saxon race. . . .

Name: _____ Date: _____

Document Analysis Worksheet

1. Date/Author of Document/Author's Position: Intended Audience:

2. Why was this document written? List three points the author made that you find important.

3. List two things the document tells you about life in the United States at the time it was written.

4. Write a question to the author that the document left unanswered.

Name: _____ Date: _____

Comparative Analysis Worksheet

Choose two documents from this week's readings in which the document authors present different takes on a particular issue.

    1. Identify two or three key points on which the authors agree and/or disagree.

_____

_____

_____

_____

_____

_____

    2. Develop your analysis of these two documents further by answering one or two questions listed in the "Questions to Consider" section for each document.

_____

_____

_____

_____

_____

_____

_____

_____

_____

_____